THE ROYAL FINE ART COMMISSION

A New Look for London

Judy Hillman

London   Her Majesty's Stationery Office

ISBN 0 11 752135 3

The Royal Fine Art Commission
initiated *A New Look for London* in
the summer of 1987 and asked Judy
Hillman to research and write a report.
The result of her work has now been
considered by the Commission and
approved for publication.

Contents

Small parades
Absentee landlords
Empty property
Anglicised strips
Urban design competitions

Speed humps or sleeping policemen
Throttle or choke
Blips
Central strips
Narrowed streets, widened pavements
Chicane
Shared surface
Temporary road closure
Subways
Parking control
Pedestrian priority

Major new green areas
Existing open space
Some London initiatives
Local involvement
Wildlife and ecology
Leftover land
A permanent gardens exhibition
Urban trails
Capsules of history
Joint borough projects

Recapturing waterfronts
A new national park
Major Thameside facilities
The Opportunities
Need for special organisation
Possible framework for action
The role

ACKNOWLEDGEMENTS

A New Look for London has greatly benefited from the ideas and advice offered by members of the Royal Fine Art Commission. A steering group was set up consisting of Dame Elizabeth Chesterton, Sir Alec Gordon, James Sutherland and Sherban Cantacuzino, the Commission's Secretary, and I would particularly like to thank them and the Chairman, Lord St. John of Fawsley, for their continuing interest and encouragement.

At the end of the report there is an appendix listing the large number of organisations, or more accurately their representatives, who contributed much information and many ideas. I am grateful to all, especially professional officers involved in planning, transport, public services and cleansing in London boroughs across the political spectrum. Very early on I wrote to all 32 boroughs and the City Corporation asking for details of experiments or pilot projects or areas in which the administrative system could benefit from change. Many individuals from different departments replied and later spent time and trouble explaining what they were doing, why and wherein lay some of the problems. While final responsibility for the report must rest with me, their generosity of time, expertise and examples of good practice has made all the difference.

The London borough of Sutton very kindly lent photographs of local initiatives. I took the rest.

Judy Hillman
July 1988

FOREWORD BY THE PRIME MINISTER

The present urban and economic renaissance provides a splendid spur for making our cities more attractive places in which to work, live and enjoy time off. The Royal Fine Art Commission plays an important role in focusing attention on issues which affect the quality of British life. I am especially glad therefore, both as a citizen and Prime Minister, to support the Commission in its campaign to achieve a new look for London.

London stands at the heart of this great nation, and its well-being is vital to us all. It is the hub of our political, financial and business life, a major centre for the arts, shopping and sport, home to nearly seven million people and a magnet to many more who come as visitors from other parts of this country and from all over the world. Architecturally the capital offers a treasure trove of buildings, new as well as old, not to mention its web of villages, squares, and parks and its panoramas, particularly along the Thames. They must be properly maintained and enhanced. If London is to retain its reputation as 'the flower of cities all' (to quote William Dunbar), it must present a public face to match its historic heritage and traditions.

A New Look for London presents some of the capital's obvious problems and offers more than 100 positive ideas for their resolution. Indeed, although it has concentrated on the capital, the issues and much of the approach are of relevance to urban living in towns and cities throughout the land. I particularly welcome the emphasis on the need for everyone – individuals and groups as well as councils – to involve themselves in the upkeep and improvement of their local streets and centres.

The report contains a number of other interesting proposals which affect many organisations including London's local authorities as well as central government departments. While some may need further investigation, I hope that *A New Look for London* will launch the beginning of renewed effort and renewed pride and concentrate attention in all areas on ideas for action – now.

July 1988

Summary

Too much of London has become dirty, degrading and depressing. Under foot litter abounds, scattered by people and the wind from pavements to streets and forecourts, often dumped hours in advance of collection or simply left in plastic parcels at the foot of almost any vertical object. Meanwhile the men, women and children, for whom the city exists, are squashed onto pavements narrowed by guard rails, bollards, grey poles, lampposts, telephone, letter, litter and traffic light control boxes, salt and grit containers, bus stops and shelters, public conveniences, trees, sometimes in tubs, and a few plants. Visually streets have become a nightmare, a situation which is compounded by a proliferation of yellow lines, yellow flashings, signs, usually dirty, estate agency boards, graffiti and flyposting.

If a wizard could wave a wand to whisk dirt, waste and clutter off the face of London, the effect would be miraculous. However, while urban magicians are scarce, there is absolutely no reason why the city should tolerate this decline in the quality of the environment. Improvement will however require popular pressure and involvement, political will and imagination.

Litter can be tackled, dirt removed, new ideas tried out, as is already happening in some parts of the capital. For example many areas need more, better designed litter bins, which are emptied on a regular basis. But this need not necessarily create additional demands on the public purse. Individuals and business can sponsor them, individuals and business can arrange to empty them. Personal responsibility should similarly be extended to the upkeep and sweeping of local pavements, the imposition of conditions on new fast food outlets and agreements with other shopkeepers and residents. After all, since the look of the local environment can affect trade and house prices, it is to everyone's advantage to begin to show more direct interest.

For noticeable all-round improvement, the quality of London life needs to be placed at the top of the local political agenda. This means the establishment in local authorities of a committee with a structure which emphasises that committee's overriding importance and coordinates the budgets and personnel of different departments to achieve systematic upgrading of the environment. It also means local collaboration – hotlines for complaints, inquiries and ideas, working parties to arouse enthusiasm, longer-term plans and cash, or sponsorship for joint action. Equally there should be rewards for members of those communities who really contribute to community care – from prizes and annual thank-you parties to more formal arrangements for quid pro quo reductions in rates or the community charge.

Local members of amenity societies, who often have relevant professional qualifications, could help in campaigns to improve the street scene by carrying out necessary local environmental audits. They could also combine their skills and good will with town hall officials to remove surplus signage and dross and give the freedom of unencumbered pavements back to people. Guard rails, if necessary, do not have to look like barricades. Metal poles do not have to be painted in a statutory shade of grey. Signs do not have to be grubby and illegible. Exterior decoration is as important as interior to personal comfort and morale – and London pride.

Such solutions will mean changes in individual and community habits as well as civic practice and administration. They will depend on the extent to which individuals, in business and other organisations, care about their city, in whole or in part. They will depend on whether people are prepared, not only to press Members of Parliament and local councils for action, but also to contribute time, ideas, effort and cash themselves to the improvement of the urban scene. And they will of course require the willingness of local politicians and officers to listen and cooperate – to eliminate the traditional gap between 'them' and 'us'.

Working together Londoners could quickly make their mark on the 620 square miles in which some seven million people have their being – the cobweb of avenues, streets, roads, crescents and squares which engulfed historic villages, towns and English countryside over the centuries. As well as tackling problems of litter, dirt, scruff and clutter, much can be done to improve town centres and reduce the overwhelming impact of traffic to give priority for people. New open space can be created, not simply by greening unused sites but also by making the streets themselves more attractive – including the addition of more trees, flowers, colour and works of art.

The Thames and its banks could be transformed into a new national park. River transport could increasingly link the existing necklace of historic sites, museums and cultural activities with places to eat, drink and shop and oases of open space. The basic framework and ingredients for this new urban park already exist. All that is needed is a small streamlined organisation to coordinate the many interests and exploit the potential, including encouraging the redevelopment of the remaining derelict sites.

But London also needs more effective Londonwide organisations which are concerned with the city's future. Even before the abolition of the Greater London Council and the creation of the amorphous London Planning Advisory Committee, there was a need for an independent London lobby or pressure group to assess the impact of development proposals and ensure that major issues are widely understood and discussed. And like cities in the United States and other parts of Britain it needs a forum for the influential – a London Looks Forward or a London 2000 – to consider ideas for creating a better, and incidentally a more internationally competitive, environment.

A New Look for London is meant to be practical. Neither an architectural nor an aesthetic blueprint, it sets out to provide ideas for action, many of which could have an immediate effect. Cities are constantly involved in an evolutionary process of decay and regeneration and London is currently witnessing massive developments which are transforming for example docklands and the City. In addition major transport proposals, including the new rail link to Heathrow, the Channel Tunnel rail terminal and a new bridge in east London, are bound to trigger further ripples of change.

But while such new projects and proposals will hopefully enchance the environment in the long term, much of their immediate impact will be local. A New Look for London, on the other hand, concerns the capital as a whole. It suggests ways in which the urban scene, which is the backcloth to so many people's lives, can be improved – now. And although the focus of interest has been confined to London, the general approach could be equally relevant elsewhere.

Of course Londoners and their leaders can go about their business and pleasure and continue to ignore the all too obvious degradation of the environment. Or they can become more responsible and responsive within their own communities at work and home and create pressure for change – by government and by themselves. Cities do not, any more than gardens, look after themselves. If this urban garden is unkempt, overgrown and gives displeasure, there must be changes in methods, management and style. There is a choice. Increasing public squalor? Or a new look for London and a more livable city?

1 Litter disgrace

The problem of litter is there for all to see – and normally ignore. Squashed cans jostle with old newspapers in street gulleys. Ubiquitous black plastic sacks and shopping bags surround litter bins and lampposts spilling forth peel, cabbage stalks, cotton wool and scrumpled packaging as faulty fastening gives way, or dogs scratch out the odd tasty treasure. The sodden mattress, broken chair, supermarket trolley, all languish by the roadside. More cast-offs and rubbish accumulate under otherwise pristine advertising hoardings, in forecourts of empty property, on cleared sites – indeed anywhere convenient. It almost seems as if litter breeds litter as society sweeps its refuse into the public domain, which is of course someone else's business, instead of under the traditional carpet, or even better a suitable receptacle indoors.

The problem has undoubtedly worsened in recent years. Every day in Westminster in the peak summer season street sweepers collect 90 tons of litter, casually dropped by people en route for business or pleasure. Indeed more than 10 per cent of this one borough's refuse is collected directly off the streets. And the amount is increasing. In a special poll relating to the borough's private Litter Bill, Westminster found that 85 per cent of people believed London had a serious litter problem and that 67 per cent of visitors thought it worse than the place in which they lived.

Lack of personal discipline is undoubtedly largely to blame. Whether or not this decline in standards out of the home stems from the permissive society, lack of parental control, bad manners or over-expectation with regard to the ability of 'them' to create and maintain a clean environment for 'us', the result is plain for all to see. London is filthy, worse than comparable cities in mainland Europe. The same is true of Britain as a whole, as children chuck away sweet papers and iced lolly wrappings and adults calmly wind down car windows and dispatch empty cans as well as squashed paper and packets as they speed to their presumably well kept homes or places of work.

The effect of such careless behaviour has been intensified by changes in spending power and lifestyle which have greatly increased the potential for litter and refuse in London's streets. Nowadays people do have more money in their pockets and they spend more on eating out – literally. Fast, sometimes labelled junk, food is popular, outlets have mushroomed throughout the city and any former inhibitions about satisfying hunger or quenching thirst in the street have long since died. There is also an increasing tendency for people to graze in and around shopping centres and markets – a plastic cup of soup from one stall or shop, followed by another of chile con carne bought further along the road, followed perhaps by a napkin-clad pastie and later a piece of sticky cake and a tangerine, all eaten on the move. Litter bins have to be very prevalent to attract the consequent debris of half-eaten morsels, paper boxes and greasy bags. They also have to be emptied more regularly. Taken with the increased level of packaging and single sheets of advertisements thrust into hand, tucked into magazines or slipped under windscreens, the sources of new waste become more than obvious.

Even so there are areas where such litter is only the unsavoury icing to an even greater problem – that produced by businesses which stack sacks and boxes on the pavement long before the collection vehicle is due or simply dump their refuse illegally in the knowledge that someone sometime will take it away. Part of the difficulty can arise because new uses in existing buildings produce more rubbish than their storage facilities can cope with. Sometimes wine bars, shops and restaurants

The illegal dumping of plastic sacks and other rubbish has almost created a new trademark for London

are simply not prepared to sacrifice the necessary square feet of potential selling space to house refuse and the public pavement becomes their dumping ground instead.

Commercial waste is different from household rubbish in that its collection is not included in the rates. Under the 1936 *Public Health Act,* a consolidation of existing acts which remains law to this day and still includes a provision for the removal of night soil, councils should make a separate charge for trade refuse. Since some trades do not see why this should be the case, they try to avoid paying anyone. For years the definition of the word 'trade' caused confusion and some councils did in fact collect, as part of their service on the rates, from cafes and restaurants or companies which produced no more refuse than the normal household. However, the 1974 *Control of Pollution Act* provided more exact definitions and, when Westminster wished to provide a 'free' collection for local business, which pays among the highest rates in the land, its attempt was barred by law.

Esoteric this may seem but the net result has been that some companies make their own arrangements with the local council or private contractors and others do not, although of course they should. They simply sneak black or green sacks into the street, a local dark corner or someone else's official refuse pile and, unless or until they are caught, rejoice in personal saving at the cost of general public squalor.

Residential areas also suffer nowadays from the lack of proper storage for household rubbish, even if they do benefit from regular collections on the rates. In times gone by, people living in London's terraces, even in rooming houses, managed to keep rubbish out of sight under the pavement or in bins in a courtyard to the rear. Social and economic change has however led to the division of many such houses into separate flats, the space under the pavement has become a bathroom or workspace and many people prefer to put out their rubbish on collection days or more frequently to avoid keeping decay indoors. Bins, when used, are often left on the street by refuse collectors or owners and often lose their lids. And of course these changes have taken place at a time when the sheer quantity of refuse has soared.

Simultaneously local responsibility has vanished with few people bothering even to sweep away dangerous snow, let alone pick up litter or dog faeces or wash down their section of the street. Yet technically although the highway (and that includes footpaths) may be public, most properties have land rights up to the middle of the road. However the postwar ethos encouraged people to expect others to look after the so-called public domain and increasingly entertainment in the home, mainly in the form of television, has made it easier to turn a blind eye on scruffy streets outside.

The disposal of bulky items provides an additional problem as a more affluent consumer society throws out more old stoves, fridges and sofas. Councils will usually collect such outworn objects for a fee and provide a civic amenity centre for people who are able and willing to bring such surplus by car, if it will fit under the hatchback or in the boot. But many people find it quicker and easier to dump their discards on some street corner or derelict site. This is equally true of worn-out cars or unwanted supermarket trolleys.

Flytipping is much the same problem in a more commercial form. Builders do not wish to pay to dump rubble, let alone drive any distance to official sites, and some will take advantage of any deserted land suitable to their purpose.

What then can be done?

LITTER AND REFUSE

Household dustbins

Dustbins now live permanently on so many streets or front door steps that their design, perhaps colour, needs new thought. Sponsors should be found for a competition, possibly organised by the Design Council, to consider solutions to the problem.

Litter bins

An occasional slim box clamped to the odd lamppost may have seemed adequate in the days when people rarely had more to discard than a cigarette packet or sweet paper. But now that high streets and squares have become outdoor dining and reading rooms, they need to be furnished with large numbers of waste paper baskets into which trash can be thrown. A number of boroughs including Westminster and Camden have shown the difference that mass provision of bins can make. They have also demonstrated that costs can be more than offset by business sponsorship. Westminster manages to make a profit on sponsored bins which is spent on environmental improvements, yet more litter bins, anti-litter publicity, additional flower beds and an annual get-together or celebration for members of helpful associations. Nevertheless bins still overflow. They need regular emptying. In Oxford Street some 450 bins are emptied a minimum of five times a day. And while neon

*Many bins are totally inadequate or
left unemptied*

Bins need to be well designed, sturdy and frequent

lime green and orange may help bring these new *objets non d'art* to immediate public attention, there is a strong case for bins which are better designed – large, easy to empty, sturdy and in keeping with their individual neighbourhood. They may cost more initially, but general appearance is part of the sales pitch of shopping centres and even residential areas when the individual wants to sell a house or flat. In addition, business, personal or community sponsorship should be possible within specified design guidelines including graphics.

Communal street bins

In the meantime, since many people do dump on the street and pavement because of lack of storage, London boroughs could well copy those continental cities which not only furnish streets with litter bins and baskets (often fixed to walls) but also more substantial lidded container boxes on wheels. These are quite big enough for a goodly number of sacks. Westminster is to experiment along these lines in Pimlico. Hammersmith and Fulham has looked at the idea but opted for additional litter bins and clearance. Perhaps some people would sneak in their business rubbish instead of hiring a contractor as officially required by law. There could also be

In mainland Europe, such containers stand at regular intervals on the street for the disposal of rubbish

protests at the design and siting of the new covered carts. But such containers do not have to be ugly and they can be painted in a local street livery.

So far as residential areas are concerned bins on wheels or some other purpose-designed container at street corners could help offset the very real problem of storage in areas where terraced property has been converted into flats. There may be a NIMBY problem as households try to ensure they are Not In My Back Yard (or rather not on my front pavement). But surely it would be far better to have the neighbours's rubbish gathered together in a lidded box than clustered by railings or under a lamppost or tree.

Local responsibility

More shopkeepers, particularly those in fast food, but even the more obviously respectable bank or building society cash point, should accept responsibility for clearing their own local bins and sweeping their sections of pavement. In Oxford Street, the operator of a number of Wimpy outlets has introduced its own street clean-up service complete with barrow. Beside Westminster Cathedral McDonald's regularly sweeps up and removes litter from the piazza. Madame Tussaud's pays the council for an extra sweeper to work full time in its area, while Peachey Property sponsors two additional employees in Carnaby Street. St. Christopher's Place also pays extra to the council for extra attention. All these companies understand that surrounding squalor will damage their image and that a practical demonstration of local pride will do it good – and could be reflected in turnover. Incidentally there is a hospital in Lancashire which runs its boiler system on local hamburger packaging as well as medical waste.

Cleansing as part of planning

Westminster has begun to use Section 52 planning agreements as a means of placing some responsibility for keeping pavements clean in the immediate vicinity of takeaway food outlets. While such arrangements require mutual cooperation and there could be problems if the original applicant is replaced, this approach begins once again to put responsibility for local upkeep back onto the occupants of individual premises. And it seems only sensible that, where possible, the source of much urban litter, and indirectly their customers through the till, should pay to clear up the mess – not the community as a whole.

As a deal with the local authority

Croydon has agreements with a number of shopkeepers that they will keep their private forecourts swept (and often those of neighbours) in return for the collection of an equivalent number of refuse sacks or bins. If the sweeping extends to the public part of the pavement, the council takes notice and is pleased. After all the place looks better. An attempt to reintroduce the concept of personal responsibility of property owners and occupiers for pavement cleanliness in residential areas on the basis of a quid pro quo reduction in rates or community charge might also pay dividends. Even without such a sweetener, some residents in Highgate, Haringey could not bear the filth any more and have set up a working party which occasionally sweeps local streets. It has negotiated an agreement with the council for the collection of the subsequent piles of rubbish.

Clean teams and city chars

Londoners and visitors are likely to become more aware of the consequences of their slovenliness if they see other individuals cleaning up on a regular basis. Tat attracts tat is a truism but it is equally true that most people are thoughtless and, like small children, hope to get away with wrongdoing and/or trust that someone else will clear up after them. If that someone is obvious, the normally adult majority may think twice before deliberately spoiling that bit of the environment. For the same reason, it helps if the men and women who sweep streets and clear bins (often different teams) stand out in the crowd. Distinctive smart clean uniforms and carts also help raise status and bring cleanliness into higher profile. In the dirtiest areas, clean teams or squads, even possibly city chars, could blaze their way through on a regular clean-up.

The presence of road sweepers can encourage people to put litter in bins

Litter abatement officer and litter watch

Bromley has established a number of litter watch areas and has a specific litter abatement officer, who meets residents and neighbourhood associations to discuss problems and possible action and generally raise the level of interest in the area's cleanliness. Window litter watch signs are a possibility together with a reporting system for offenders. So far of course the keen are the converted. While there are staff implications in extending the scheme, nevertheless results so far have shown that, given the lead, people are prepared to become more involved and help themselves.

Information

People need information about the date and time of refuse collections

Councils could do more in the way of letting ratepayers know about practice and the law – when their collections take place, how long beforehand they can leave refuse on the highway, how it should be bagged or parcelled, whom to contact if there is a problem or, even better, what individuals can do for themselves. But the information needs to be snappily designed. Westminster has produced cards with details of refuse collections on one side (e.g. properly sealed plastic sacks should only be placed out for collection half an hour before the stated times) and street cleansing on the other. It also includes telephone numbers for people to use to report abandoned vehicles, oil spillage and, under the heading street watch, such items as builders skips, tables and chairs, advertising and estate agents boards, illegal trading and flyposting. Simply including information in an article in a free borough magazine is unlikely to achieve the desired end since many must be thrown away unread and, even if they are read, torn-out flimsy sheets are not the easiest form of reference material to keep readily to hand.

Hotline networks

Telephone hotlines for the urban consumer can also become a positive part of an information network to improve the quality of the environment. In Oxford Street Westminster has set up a system whereby shopkeepers are asked to act as the eyes and ears of the council and have key telephone numbers to contact when problems, for example overflowing litter bins, occur. This sort of relationship takes time and effort to develop but a start can be made through street associations. And in these days of mobile telephones, good management should be able to ensure the message gets through to the men or women on the clean beat.

Local posters

Kensington and Chelsea fixes red and black posters to trees and lampposts warning people they can be fined up to £200 if they leave litter underneath. One notice says: 'The litter bin that was sited here for the benefit of passing pedestrians to deposit their litter has been removed due to the inconsiderate and unacceptable abuse by people using the litter bin and surrounding pavement as a household refuse tip.' Another: 'Do not dump rubbish around this tree. It is environmental vandalism and an offence.'

On-the-spot fixed penalties

Since people take time to learn new habits and often need sticks as well as carrots to encourage the process, Westminster's recent litter legislation could provide the necessary threat to provoke better behaviour. About 70 officers (including street and cleansing inspectors but not street sweepers) have been authorised, as they go about their business in the borough, to ask individuals seen dropping or placing litter to pick it up. If they refuse, the officers can issue on-the-spot £10 fixed penalty tickets, which have to be paid – like parking fines – within a set period. If people do not pay up, then legal processes come into play which, on conviction, can lead to a maximum fine of £400. In the first three months up to mid June, the system of challenge seemed to have worked, in that more than 200 people immediately acceded to the request to bend down and pick up the offending scraps of paper. Only one ticket had been issued. As with clean-ups, there may be a case for the well advertised and obvious blitz, with groups of officers out and about, ready to issue cautions and tickets. Heavyhanded it may seem at the beginning but London's face is part of its fortune and somehow the message has to be brought home. Westminster has also introduced uniformed zone improvement patrols (ZIPs), who do move in on defined areas to tackle a series of environmental and enforcement problems. If such environmental officers should become the equivalent of an urban patrol force which supplements the police and whose very presence, like teachers, encourages better urban manners, so much the better.

Prosecution and publicity

Some boroughs like Brent and Kensington and Chelsea tackle areas where dumping occurs and sort through bags for evidence to track down urban criminals. Current litter legislation is often sadly of little help as councils have to name the actual person who does the dumping and cannot simply prosecute the source. It is also almost impossible to seize a person as they deposit rubbish and witnesses tend to be unwilling to give evidence.

Kensington and Chelsea has developed a sophisticated warning and prosecution system using the 1980 Highways Act. The Director of Engineering and Works

Westminster officers can issue fixed penalty tickets if people are seen dropping litter and refuse to pick it up – but many offenders have yet to be caught

Services sends photocopies of identification material from rubbish to property owners inviting an explanation of alleged offences. He also warns them that, depending on their reply, a report may be forwarded to the borough solicitor. In one blitz on the Kings Road, businesses which had contracts with the council for refuse removal were also reminded of collection days and told the earliest time they could put bags out. 'Under the *Highways Act 1980* it is an offence to place refuse on the highway albeit it is deemed reasonable to do so just prior to refuse collections being made,' they were told. 'You are not permitted to use the pavement or roadway as a refuse storage area and an enforcement campaign is underway to report illegal refuse dumpers for prosecution.' Other businesses received a similar letter and were asked to ensure that refuse was not placed outside more than one hour before any expected collection time. When the council prosecutes, it makes sure that firms and fines are published.

Not only do fines need to be high enough to deter but costs sufficient to cover the true expense of the process. Even in the most efficient of councils this is obviously much higher than many magistrates think. But why should other Londoners, rather than the offender, have to pay for prosecution costs taken on their behalf?

When councils are successful in court, they should, like Kensington and Chelsea, release details to the media. Most firms and individuals would quite naturally prefer to keep their misdemeanours quiet when they cheat on society's rules for playing the urban game.

Recycling

As well as sensible conservation of the earth's resources, recycling can reduce some forms of litter. The economics and legal requirements vary in different countries. For example in Quebec, Canada children supplement pocket money by collecting and returning cans and bottles for the original few cents of deposit. In Japan it is normal for households to separate waste into separate bags for different days with special collections of waste paper which qualify for free supplies of household paper products such as table napkins and toilet paper.

In Britain in a number of areas, including South Glamorgan, Leeds, Bristol and Bath, major recycling schemes have been organised, usually by the voluntary sector in cooperation with the local authority. Birmingham has launched a company to collect glass, aluminium cans and paper in supermarkets, shopping centres and car parks with profits dedicated to the local children's hospice appeal. In London there are a number of recycling centres and an increasing number of bottle banks, with, in Westminster, a special bottle bus which calls on restaurants. Provided receptacles are well designed, sensibly located, regularly emptied and kept clean, such enterprises can help the look and wellbeing of London. But a bottle bank should not be allowed to become a bottle dump. Camden reckons 63 per cent of the contents of the average dustbin could be salvaged if householders and business sorted waste at source. In Mole Valley, Surrey, one school collects waste paper to pay for the heating of its swimming pool. The same area has two big canisters for bottles in every car park. London has a recycling forum but there is still enormous scope for more experiments and activity. On the basis that litter should be tackled at source, deposits on cans and bottles could provide some incentive for the return of empties and for children to collect extra pocket money from the highways and byways.

Education

Last but not least, children need to be taught in the home, as well as at school, to clear up their litter and that of other people, even to the point of politely returning items to the original owner if they see something dropped in the street. So far as the adult population is concerned, there needs to be a concerted drive to waken people's consciousness and sense of personal responsibility, combined with the stick of public ignominy and fines.

BULKY ITEMS

Old stoves, broken chairs and mattresses present a different problem. Many people do not have cars to take decrepit household castoffs to the nearest official centre, others do not want to and neither may wish to pay the local council for personal collection, if they can unload dead or unwanted furniture and possessions in the middle of the night.

However there are a number of ways of tackling this problem. Lewisham has a free bookable lumber collection service. Kensington and Chelsea also provides a free household removal service for up to 10 bulky items on request. Brent arranges with local associations to locate covered skips temporarily and the association then passes on the good news to people living in the area. This works quite well – the main problem being canny builders and do-it-yourself enthusiasts who happily unload rubble as well as rubbish to save time and trouble. In Tower Hamlets Wapping has considered sponsorship of more permanent skips by local business to pay for the cost of the extra service. And Bromley has proved that Londoners are only too happy to latch onto the convenience of a special area door-to-door service, when they picked up 95 tonnes of unwanted furniture, cookers, fridges and garden rubbish in a one-off trial.

Unwanted household furniture is dumped in the street – or on vacant sites

In Toronto Canada they do things even better. On a regular night each week during the summer months, people put out bulk garbage, which means that household treasure seekers can roam the streets and remove suitable but rejected objects. The next morning the city collection service picks up the remnants. In Germany a similar system operates once a month. This must be a good idea for a similar experiment here.

SUPERMARKET TROLLEYS

Supermarket and station trolleys are so useful that some people like to push their purchases all the way home. Some children find them more exciting than roller skating and therefore again remove them from their official base. Whatever their use however, such trolleys all too rarely find their way back and lie forgotten in some cul-de-sac or other public place.

More supermarkets should consider the introduction of a deposit system of at least £1 to provide a reasonable incentive, even if the vehicle strays, for children to wheel them back for the extra cash. Trolleys are expensive and the cost of replacing the strays simply puts prices up in the shops.

Abandoned Cars

Dead cars are depressing neighbours. They not only take much needed parking space but open the street to other forms of litter, vandalism and general abuse as human vultures remove the better mechanical pickings. In London councils have to approach Swansea Vehicle Licensing Centre for the owner's name and address, then write, write again and finally fix a warning notice for a month's set period before the car is finally removed and crushed. Since the whole process can take between three and six months, it would surely be simpler if a request to Swansea was made at the same time as a warning was pasted onto a car reported as abandoned by local residents. The vehicles could then be removed to a compound for a further fixed period where owners would pay a fixed penalty for their recovery, as is already the case for cars towed away for parking offences.

Public rubbish on private land

In the ideal world private ownership implies private care. In the real world, particularly if a building or site is empty, owners, whether individuals or organisations, worry little about appearance unless damage could affect values and their pockets. Because the public domain, especially the public highway, is not affected, councils tend to look the other way until complaints become too vociferous, the reputation of an area, and perhaps investment, is at stake or the threat or actuality of rats and decay raises health issues.

The planning law enables councils to trace land owners, serve notice giving them time to take action and then, if they do not comply, to send in a clean-up squad and forward the bill. But the process can be slow and, if the problem recurs, has to be repeated from the start. Councils ought to be able to serve a notice directly onto the property giving due warning, then clear up the mess and send a full bill when they manage to trace the owner, covering adminstrative costs as well as those of rubbish removal, each time the job has to be done.

Councils do sometimes simply order their contractors to cope automatically with bad sites. And one London borough has occasionally taken a different sort of direct action against individual companies and statutory undertakers. It sends a photograph and short letter to chief executives expressing confidence that they personally are ignorant of the problem and assuming that they will of course immediately remedy the situation to improve their local public image. This method has worked well and is worth copying. Advertising hoardings often stand with their feet in litter along the highway edge and advertisers may feel less than efficiently handled if expensive poster campaigns and their reputation by association are tarnished by tatty locations. A letter and photograph of the state of the setting of their advertisements might lead to direct commercial pressure on agents to look after their sites. The encouragement of local newspapers to campaign against offenders and publish pictures of the worst sites with full details of ownership might also be a good idea.

FLYTIPPING

Flytipping sounds such mild civic abuse – a fly is small, fly-by-night temporary and exciting rather than the potentially permanent and offensive eyesore this urban crime has become. For crime it is to steal private and public open space in London for rubble, scrap and earth from building sites which by right should fill a gaping hole in the home counties. But of course tippers can make more money if

(1) they dump their load for free in town, whereas they may have to pay for the privilege outside and turn up within fixed hours; and

(2) they travel a much shorter distance – for example to Southwark instead of Medway so allowing perhaps 10 instead of two return trips a day.

Building and rebuilding activity in the capital has increased and flytipping is a constant problem, particularly in Southwark, Lewisham, Greenwich and the East End. Deserted spots, preferably isolated from public view, provide the best targets and the councils have at times found roads as well as pavements and accessible empty sites, suddenly piled high with rubble.

To catch flytipping cowboys is difficult, even if the police are involved. Subsequent prosecution is complex and involves the tracing of number plates (which may be false) to the owner, who by law has to say who was responsible. Quite frequently the owner is new, having acquired the vehicle since the offence. While there have been successful prosecutions, fines could well be increased substantially even to begin to dent the potential profits and attraction of such operations. The London Waste Regional Authority has been pressing for additional realistic compensation to cover the cost of removal of the solid material.

WATERWAYS

The Thames presents special problems in that the Thames Water Authority and the Port of London Authority are basically responsible for the cleanliness of the water but sometimes show less interest in the foreshore. Local authorities have no statutory duty for its upkeep but Hammersmith and Fulham for example does look after those areas where there is a river walk and has occasionally used urban programme money to provide skips for voluntary weekend clean-ups. The PLA now has a scheme for catching driftwood but the cleanliness of the banks of the Thames matters so much to London pride and enjoyment that it should not be left to chance. Responsibility needs to be assigned with suitable sanctions to ensure the job is carried out.

London's canals are also plagued with drifting litter and need much more cooperation between British Waterways Board, councils and local commercial interests to ensure proper maintenance. One attempt by the company running the market at Camden Lock to skim off the worst of the sodden dross ran at least temporarily into union problems. Although the work was hardly ever tackled, its management was told it was taking away people's jobs. The company does however maintain a length of towpath.

THE LONDON UNDERGROUND

Finally there is the appearance of the London Underground, in particular the stations. London Regional Transport is presumably in the business of providing regular, reliable, quick, comfortable, safe journeys to people. It is selling a service essential to the capital's residents and commuters and a major facility for visitors from home and abroad. However in an age when general image increasingly counts, LRT's all too frequent slovenly appearance offsets other improvements, including refurbished stations. Its top management simply has to make it look as if the organisation actually tries. Difficult though the task may be to cope with thousands of trampling feet, tunnel dust, litter, vandalism and graffiti, other marketing organisations – for example shopping centres – manage. A survey by the Department of Transport on crime on the underground showed that passengers found even the sight of graffiti symptomatic of a wider lack of supervision and contributed to their feelings of insecurity on the system. Most regular passengers can probably name their unfavourite black spot, such as the approach to the Northern Line at Leicester Square (an otherwise modernised station) which was remarkable for at least six months in 1987 for dirt and graffiti-filled empty advertising space.

Even with more than 250 stations, it should surely be possible to give every single one a regular spring-clean, scraping and scrubbing off dirt. Regular daily cleaning should also be visible in the hope that people will be less likely to drop litter if another human being is actually cleaning nearby. While LRT has been looking at its cleaning arrangements, the London Regional Passengers Committee reckons that every station should be clean each day when the system opens. 'We have said you may well require fewer people to operate the underground in terms of modern technology but if society changes as it has, so that everything you buy comes in masses and masses of packaging, then you have to provide the staff levels necessary and the size of waste paper baskets necessary to meet the changed circumstances and pay for that,' says the secretary, Rufus Barnes.

2 More scruff and dirt

But the problem is not just litter. Other types of scruff and dirt make the capital look unkempt and depress people's spirits as they do their daily rounds.

GRAFFITI

While London has examples of inventive, even attractive spray painting, disfiguring graffiti is much the more common form of self expression. London Transport again suffers horribly. A brand new bus once had to be taken out of service after two hours and required the equivalent of one man working steadily for four days to put it back in business. Other problem areas include subways, ill-designed areas of urban residential wilderness and almost any convenient blank stone or painted wall.

Some remedies

Apart from swift removal to avoid a build-up, there are remedies for many blank walls – murals, preferably involving local people working with an artist, or, as in a Bromley experiment, the addition of a wooden trellis, creeper and other planting to cover the wall and make it less accessible. There may be a case for providing local graffiti walls which teenagers can spray and respray and the installation of legal commercial poster sites can also sometimes be an answer.

Graffiti rarely improves the environment

Bromley planted a climbing shrub to cover an inviting blank wall near the shopping centre and discourage graffiti

Murals can contribute to street vitality as well as provide another form of cover-up

London Underground

London Underground has plans to fill empty advertising hoardings with LRT's own posters. The sooner, the better. But perhaps LRT could also develop posters aimed at reducing litter and vandalism – admonition, education and details of successful prosecutions. It could also offer empty space on a temporary basis to charities. At present empty holes on the wall are an invitation to unwanted scribblers.

And what about more sales kiosks at subterranean interchanges and on platforms? In the Paris Metro they provide a service, add vitality and colour, create a generally more secure environment and provide extra cash flow.

Subways

In subways more generally, anti-graffiti surfaces, possibly including a tiled mural, can help. Controlled circuit television is a useful deterrent to vandals – and mugging – and Hammersmith and Fulham have now found ways of keeping the costs of installation and monitoring to a reasonable level.

In the ideal world, the culprits would be caught and, as at least part of the punishment, return to the scene and literally clean up their crime. At the very least the convicted graffiti offender should pay the full cost of removal as happens for example in Vancouver.

In Britain however the law does not give graffiti a high crime rating. Yet, as secretary of the London Regional Passengers Committee, Rufus Barnes, says: 'The impact it has on morale and people generally and the look of London actually makes it quite serious.' Magistrates have no power to make young offenders convicted of graffiti or litter crimes spend time on a capital clean-up. While community service may seem the obvious avenue and the Government has emphasised its use to improve the appearance and quality of neighbourhoods including the removal of graffiti, it is only an option for older offenders, can only be awarded with the offender's agreement and the probation service, not the court, decides what form the service to the community will take.

While the Government should make it possible for courts to decide if the offender's service should relate to the original environmental crime, that would still not involve younger vandals who cannot be sent to prison and therefore do not qualify for community service. Fines in such cases – a maximum of £100 for criminal proceedings against children aged 10 to 13 and of £400 for those between 14 and 16 – are often irrelevant. For some, intermediate treatment is a possibility but this comes under the control of social workers and, even though it could take the form of clearing up, they tend to opt for reading or writing. Like the probationary service, they see themselves in a more caring and advisory role. Obviously sensitivity is needed but there is a case for some children also to be awarded a punishment which better fits the crime and even involves their parents in removing the mess. Courts can, but rarely do, fine parents, partly because many are single mothers without jobs and partly because the law is unclear. Some magistrates defer cases for a short period on the basis that if the graffiti disappears in the meantime, they will take a more lenient view. This would seem a highly constructive approach.

FLYPOSTING

Flyposting is anonymous – stick and run. The poster may be perfectly well designed, the information of interest to many. But unlike official advertising, wall, lamppost and fence owners receive no income, the local authority has no opportunity to give or withold planning consent and no one makes sure the sheet is cleaned off when

Flyposted walls – out-of-date information left to rot and attract litter and graffiti

the event has taken place or the message is no longer relevant. If only such posters were self-destructive after a limited period, all would be relatively well. However the age of fixed time-degradable notices has yet to come and, like litter, one bill attracts a broadsheet which attracts a poster, which creates a mish-mash, which is then torn and/or defaced to contribute yet again to the overall impression in many parts of the city of irresponsibility, carelessness and lack of pride.

In theory it is now possible to prosecute the organisation or person who stands to gain from the notice – for example the organiser of the car boot sale or the church staging the concert. In practice such individuals can claim they knew not what was being done in their name, although this defence fails if authority issues a warning and the offending poster is not removed. While councils can themselves remove such advertisements after a short warning period, they cannot recover costs. The law should be changed so that they can.

As another means of reducing the problem, Westminster is beginning to attach anti-flyposter conditions to entertainment licences. This means that if flyposting advertising the event does take place, the organisers can run into licensing difficulties next time round.

Another idea would be to create the community equivalent of the office or kitchen pinboard with legal flyposting screens attached to railings, blank walls or even traffic signal control boxes. In addition some sites now used for flyposting might be given temporary licences for advertising so that owners would have the potential for income and a natural economic spur to keep the posters in good condition and up to date.

BLACKENED BUILDINGS

Just because a building is built of stone or concrete, that does not mean it never needs its equivalent of a coat of paint – in other words the removal of one coat or more of dirt. All too many London structures are still blanketed in the soot of yesteryear. While some people find blackened columns, frills, sills and statuary add character, as do deep-etched wrinkles to an elderly face, the cleaning of buildings around Parliament Square for example has revealed new beauty and vibrancy, which before lay concealed under urban grime. A wash and brush-up would benefit many other buildings and lift the spirit of a number of city streets.

DEBRIS AND DUST

The only cities free from problems associated with buildings and development are those which are dying or dead, the literal museum of urban history, frozen for all time as tourist attractions – and even they sometimes find they need scaffolding and maintenance. London is lucky to be a living organic capital with constant refurbishment and renewal of individual buildings, streets and whole districts.

Hoardings and screens can reduce the debris and dust of building and provide urban sparkle – or information

While improvements and development are often exciting, necessary and desirable, building works often greatly subtract, if only temporarily (which can sometimes mean for years) from a neighbourhood's quality of life. Scaffolding for major and minor sites can trespass onto the pavement, skips block off the use of street space, the storage of materials for small works is equally obstructive, cement mixing on the highway messy.

The City Corporation in 1987 launched an initiative called the Considerate Contractor Scheme which appears to have been very successful. With the explosion in new building, officers found high voltage cables trailing into the road and were repeatedly warning contractors about possible prosecution if their works affected the safety of

the public highway. Under the CCS, which was introduced in September and required the appointment of two highway surveyors, contractors become members, pledge to keep sites and local pavements tidy, and erect special hoarding boards announcing their membership, the accepted code of practice and details of a hotline for complaints. Two months later, the City was able to make nine gold awards and give merit certificates to all but 11 sites at a party to which site managers and company representatives were invited. Now companies are vying with one another over the appearance and maintenance of sites including sponging down boards and sweeping pavements. The CCS has attracted numerous inquiries from local authorities with Chelmsford and Sheffield already following the City's lead and hopefully, it should be said, other parts of London.

Elsewhere major firms have also found it pays off in terms of pride and potentially their corporate image if they dress up hoardings with simple bands of paint or murals. The developers of the Jubilee Hall site in Covent Garden paid a charitable organisation to design and adorn hoardings with local scenes – and development details. This certainly softened the impact of major disruption of this popular commercial corner. More recently the same developer brought colourful fun to a corner of Trafalgar Square with a massive painted ship's bridge. The reverse side of the building near the National Gallery has boasted another exceptional mural, treatment fitting for one of London's busiest visitor (and resident) crossroads. The pavements of Piccadilly were well protected from the effects of the London Pavilion refurbishment by a plastic screen covered with an architectural blueprint or sketch of the building. Yet when the Government commissioned necessary maintenance of Nelson on his column, there was no artistic replica. He simply vanished behind a screen with total disregard of the seasonal nature of his visiting audience and the need to consider the needs of London's tourist trade in the Whitehall refurbishment programme.

While murals or drawings of the final scheme are good public relations, it would be excessive to expect this as a universal approach. Much greater use of sheeting and rubble removal tubes would however be helpful and could form a normal environmental condition for planning and building works taking place within a specific distance of the street. London would look better and feel better for everyone who passes anywhere near.

Licences are required for scaffolding and skips which occupy part of the public highway. Perhaps it is time for local authorities to consider whether there should also be some form of hire charge when that space is temporarily removed from public use.

PATCHWORK PAVING

Rough cracked paving with patches is another major detraction from the London scene. It also happens to be dangerous. While ordinary roads, with an increasing number of potholes and strips of ridged tarmac, are bad enough, a street has only it seems to be pedestrianised, with well chosen bricks or blockwork, for some statutory undertaker to arrive, dig a trench, fill it in again and ice the final product with totally different material, probably black. Pavements are even worse. Anyone who watches closely where they walk – and everyone needs to – will enjoy a never-ending eyeful of cracked slabs and tortuous patches of all shapes and sizes leading from and along the road to individual properties. Once again the capital gives an impression of a third-rate country unable to afford proper maintenance, with citizens, civic bodies and service organisations lacking interest in their surroundings and the quality of their work. That may not be true. But local councils are trapped by out-of-date law and inefficient disinterested practice into accepting a deteriorating environment for which they are then blamed. And of course additional building and more people and businesses wanting extra services have made the situation even worse.

The present situation stems from the *Public Utilities and Street Works Act* which enables organisations like British Telecom, British Gas, Thames Water and London Electricity to provide and maintain essential and desirable services. They have to pay for the area they disturb and, under normal practice, carry out a temporary reinstatement, which explains all the patched paving. Only when they give clearance can the local authority move in and restore the pavement to its original state. There are a number of problems. The service supplier may not worry much about the ability of a particular pipelayer or mender to respect or even notice good quality paving or brick or provide a neat, if temporary, finish. Some hack out much wider areas than necessary and use the original bricks as part of the fill. In addition the self-same statutory undertaker may plan to carry out further works in due course and refuse clearance of a particular job for months, if not years. Third, even when it does get clearance, the local authority may wish to programme reinstatement with other work and wait to do several sections of the street together. And of course there are then arguments about the precise area of damage and the cost, because

Scars remain far too long after the provision and maintenance of essential services such as electricity, gas and telephone

*Better and more interesting paving
in Wandsworth, the Isle of Dogs and
the French town of Bergerac*

the service organisations dislike paying for more expensive type of paving, if not quite a gold-plated job.

Given this thoroughly unsatisfactory position, the Government set up a committee, which issued a voluminous report, and then proposed legislation, which may still place insufficient emphasis on the quality of replacement. It suggested that each organisation – and all in time may be public companies – should become legally responsible for their own repairs whenever they dig up the pavement or road. In theory this may be sensible. After all they and their customers should shoulder the full burden in terms of costs and works. However London boroughs are worried that they will not necessarily do a proper job in terms of appearance, safety and speed and, although councils may be able to put any defects to rights, they wonder who is going to judge what is or is not defective, by what criteria and who is going to pay that judge.

The answer may lie in some arrangement similar to party wall agreements. When property owners carry out construction which affects neighbouring properties, they have to pay for the appointment of independent surveyors to check on the situation before and after the work and to guarantee full repair and restoration in the event of any damage. On this basis the statutory undertakers would be required to pay local authorities a fee to inspect and approve their reinstatement. It is important that any Bill makes the pavement digger pay for this official inspectorate and that there are ways by which it can insist on full restoration within a certain period of time. It is also important that the statutory undertakers are given a proper environmental remit, so that even temporary repairs match the surrounding area – for example the same colour and quality and finished off tidily. Better standards are after all in their interest. Share prices can be affected by fair criticism and lack of environmental consideration or awareness is likely to be of increasing importance to their competitive image. If the statutory undertakers had to sign their handiwork with distinctive small studs so that people could identify the companies or organisations creating urban shoddyness, some could quickly find they were forced to take a more responsible role for the surface as well as the pipe or cable. They should not expect to get by on the cheap.

Of course it can help too if councils issue reply-paid postcards and offer hotlines for reports of problems with paving, provided they then put on pressure or take action. Such complaint cards should be made available widely in for example corner shops and supermarkets so that people who never go near town halls or libraries are aware they exist.

Dogs

Dogs may be man's best friend but they foul the London environment, particularly pavements and parks, and do not even pay a proper poll tax to cover the cost of their bad works. The faeces look unpleasant and create a serious health risk. Boroughs operate under outdated bye-laws which, even for successful prosecutions, result in ridiculously low fines. The aptly named Barking led London with the introduction of the hand-held Pooper-scooper so that dog owners can clear up any mess immediately and dispose of it in bins at park exits, a system which has been adopted by other boroughs including Kensington and Chelsea, Hounslow and Westminster. In addition new bye-laws are gradually being introduced to make the removal of dog fouling compulsory. However when Westminster suggested that owner responsibility with maximum fines raised to £100, should apply to canine pavement as well as park offenders, the Home Office backed away. Perhaps this is another area where punishment of offenders could be made to fit the crime and they should become temporary street cleaners. Dogs add to the quality of some people's life in London. They detract from others and their owners should be responsible or pay up for that privilege.

Pigeons

No one – at least only some people – would like a pigeon-free capital city. After all they provide part of the visitor attraction of Trafalgar Square and they are one of the few wild forms of life which visibly inhabit the urban scene. But collections of birds on bridges across the capital's roads result in dirt on the footpaths which can be dangerous as well as unsightly. While the boroughs can and do try to keep the pavements clean, the problem simply recurs. British Rail and London Regional Transport allow councils to net bridges but local fury can erupt when pigeons get entangled. One alternative may be the installation of anti-perch treatment – a kind of nylon bristle – to encourage birds to move on to a perch further away which does not cause the same problem.

The boroughs do not see why they should be responsible when the shape and position of someone else's property – the bridge – is the cause. 'Sometimes we have painted their bridges, cleaned their walls and abutments and provided netting and they won't accept any responsibility at all. They should be responsible,' says one borough works officer. That is right, they should be.

3 Clutter – mainly official

London's pavements have become an obstacle course. Anyone who trips over a bollard or parking meter, races along the inner track of never-ending street barriers or stops, stares and begins to count the plethora of objects must wonder if town hall bureaucrats travel only by car, hate human beings, have missed their real metier as junk shop owners or quite simply are blind. It may look like planning gone mad, with signposts and lampposts jostling bollards, bus shelters, hydrants, letter, grit and traffic control boxes, let alone telephone kiosks, litter bins, benches or trees and the above mentioned bollards and fences. But in fact there is no planning – just a host of official acts and regulations which dictate and allow different sections of the town hall and government, nationalised industries and recently privatised companies (the so-called statutory undertakers) to do virtually what they will. Add

Even in an important street like Piccadilly, the pavement boasts a cluttered profusion of signs, posts and other impedimenta

to this accumulation of good intent scaffolding, stacked building materials, dustbins, sacks of litter, the odd pub or shop billboard, edge-of-paving dips for the disabled, and the chaos is complete – until another sign goes up, perhaps welcoming visitors to the heart of London or announcing a nuclear-free zone, planted on yet more poles.

While the actual road space tends to be kept relatively clear for moving and parked vehicles, for which purpose it is presumed to exist, obviously no such presumption holds sway about the overriding need of people on foot for space in which to walk. Yet the footpath forms just as much a part of the highway as the road surface alongside and pedestrian movement just as much an essential form of transport as the car, bus, van or lorry. However with safety and speed ever uppermost in their minds, transport engineers seem all too rarely consider anything but pedestrian safety and only then in terms of contact with vehicular traffic. It is all too obvious that unobstructed movement on the footpath has no priority, that pavement collisions between people or with traffic hardware rate low in their list of concerns, if at all. It is equally obvious that the footpath is too often seen as an adjunct to the road, resulting in its insidious erosion for the benefit of traffic on wheels. And if people on foot dare to gain extra space by nipping along the gulley or crossing at corners, such initiative is quickly ended with the insertion of metal corrals to harass and discomfort their walking lives – and that includes Londoners, commuters and visitors.

The really observant recorder of the various species of urban clutter will notice that most vertical objects – such as bollards, parking meters, posts and lamposts – are set 18 inches in from the pavement edge. As well as increasing the trip-up danger to people on foot, their location reduces the traditional eight feet pavement width to less than six and a half. There is of course a reason. Lorries and other vehicles with substantial overhang might otherwise knock such obstacles regularly askew which, say engineers, would make the street look even worse. But once again vehicles benefit at the expense of people on foot.

The invasion of grey poles or posts is another important feature of the modern street. About eight feet high, basically a piece of pipe and often uncapped, they are used to support signs, sometimes single and tiny, for example, 'No parking at any time'. Sometimes grey poles can be found literally in the middle of pavements, carrying the weight of larger road signs, one-way arrows or No entry rondels. Most try to tell something to drivers of vehicles. But it is the pedestrian who has to negotiate the slalom course resulting from the accretion of impedimenta which, to be fair, also includes the offerings of other town hall departments and the statutory undertakers.

Victorian prints indicate the extent of the decline of London's pavements as outdoor corridors for purposeful movement, let alone pleasurable walking or a chance to see the buildings as a backcloth to life in a great capital city. Indeed it is amazing how councils can be financially so hard pressed and still find the cash for yet more signs, bollards and guard rails.

Of course few people would expect an absolutely clean sweep of all this modern impedimenta. After all motorists need signs, people want telephone kiosks, letter boxes and shelter as they wait for buses, even traffic lights and pedestrian crossings. And some advertising and virtually all cafe tables and chairs add to vitality and urban ambience.

But every so often in life and in cities it is necessary to step back and take a look at basic principles. While individuals tend to do this when they move house, towns should occasionally also take stock and start again. In London the time really has come to try to give pavements back to the people and help the city emerge from the undergrowth. Even within the constraints of existing traffic regulations and requirements, much can be done.

PLAN FOR ACTION

1. London boroughs should designate an officer with design qualifications with the power to vet the need and then approve the style and placing of all additional signs and other objects on public footpaths.

2. The boroughs should also select one or more streets as demonstration projects for reappraisal and a spring-clean, the main object being to remove as much clutter as possible and rearrange the rest.

3. Since finance and manpower are limited, local organisations should be encouraged to help in the research, contribute ideas and possibly help with implementation. When Richmond reviewed every sign in the town centre, the Richmond Society shared the donkeywork with the planning department and helped work out for example how to protect views. Most amenity societies have members who could

carry out the necessary census of all pavement hardware.

4. Once this necessary information is available, a small working party should be set up to include professionals from within and without the council to see what is legally necessary, decide what else is desirable and generally reorder the scene. Common sense and iconoclasm may be important in questioning and changing the status quo. The fundamental reassessment should include:

Yellow lines

Yellow lines do not have to be so wide or so bright

Are they absolutely necessary? There are experimental schemes, particularly in historic areas in other parts of the country, where parking regulations have relied on signing alone. Indeed the yellow line has no legal status. It simply warns drivers of local waiting restrictions, the details of which feature on tiny metal signs on yellow (waiting). Flashings indicate loading restrictions, for which the relevant notices are white.

Where yellow lines are helpful, it may be useful for more people to know that the Department of Transport does not quibble with two inch lines instead of three inches. (And if two inches, why not one inch?) Nor need the yellow paint be so brash. Wandsworth has used marigold for example. And indeed paint can be replaced by pale yellow tape or brick, as is the case in Neal Street and beside the Queen Elizabeth II Conference Centre in Westminster. Engineers are so concerned with safety that they often do not seem to worry about the visual impact of their measures on the urban scene. Design should be part of the remit.

Parking meters

There seems no good reason why these should so often march Indian file down the pavement edge – inset 18 inches of course – when they would occupy less space at the back. But surely it is time to question their very *raison d'etre*. In car parks all over the country people are accustomed to pay and display, buying tickets at a central box and leaving them in their car windows. Bath has introduced a scheme for pre-paid parking cards or vouchers which motorists buy in advance from local shops and garages. The vouchers are then cancelled and displayed inside cars to show arrival times. In London, with 33 local authorities interested in the income, such a system might be complicated to introduce. Hounslow is however installing more traditional pay-and-display ticket machines in Chiswick High Road and there are numerous places where a group of meters could be replaced by one or more ticket machines, preferably programmed to take pre-paid plastic (like Phonecards) and thus less likely to tempt street robbers. At the moment the inner pavement around St. James's Square for example is lost to pedestrians as is the north side of Carlton Gardens. The removal of meters in favour of fewer ticket machines could help return many pavements to people.

One pay-and-display machine – this is a French horodotaire – could replace a long file of London parking meters

Bollards

Since legislation was passed to enable boroughs to ban parking on pavements, London has sprouted concrete and wooden bollards. Bollards can be useful, they can even be quite handsome, but they too often simply add to pavement clutter and narrow the footpath. Clamping is an effective deterrent used in some parts of London which affects the motorist and leaves the pedestrian untramelled. In other areas enforcement of the law is surely a better option than the imposition of bollards, although fines should reflect the costs of bringing cases to court and of damaged paving. In Barnet in 1986 283 motorists were fined for parking on pavements but fines ranged from as low as £10 to £50 and costs from £5 to £25. One small misdeed it may seem to the offender and the court but magistrates need to understand the cumulative impact of the environmental offence on society and that people will try to get away with what they can unless they fear for their time and their pockets. Clamping has showed that the combination of nuisance and cost does make individuals more careful where they park. So could fines.

Guard rails

Are they really necessary and if so, over what distance and in what style? The numbers of people on foot are not that much greater than they were in days of yore before this mean form of urban control began to herd and crush pedestrians and make crossing streets more time-consuming and difficult, particularly at staggered layouts with push-button signals. In Kensington High Street, the council plans to build out pavements and once again enable people to take the straightest shortest route. A great deal of existing railing should simply be removed. If there are so many people that they spill out from the pavement, the answer should perhaps be wider pavements.

At the top of Haymarket, people are corralled behind railings while cars enjoy the freedom of the road

Lampposts

Lighting of all kinds can be fixed to walls

Given the likely increase of street crime in ill-lit neighbourhoods, lighting can provide a sense of security as well as the potential, as on a stage, for enhancing, even dramatising, the street. While lampposts can be good-looking, even beautiful, many are not. The City of London quite normally attaches lighting to buildings and, although the Corporation has powers to fix lights to all but Crown or Government property, it never seems to need to use them. Officers try to be diplomatic with owners and make sensible investigations to find the best, not necessarily the shortest, cable route. Fittings and brackets vary according to the neighbourhood, all wiring is covered and the cost is less than the traditional lamppost in terms of capital outlay and maintenance.

Grey poles and signs

Are they all necessary and could those which are be placed somewhere else? The stated reason for those which boast only the small sign about waiting or unloading restrictions is the possibility of failing to convict an offender in court, should signs be anything but absolutely obvious. However Wandsworth has placed some on bollards and the City Corporation tries to use buildings. Many people would prefer to allow their property to be used in this way to the arrival of a pavement post immediately outside their premises. Others should follow the lead.

In addition signs all too often outlive their usefulness or are so badly placed that they might as well not be there at all. While some are necessary under traffic legislation, even these can sometimes be relocated or grouped to impart the same information in a more orderly and even environmentally considerate way. A circular, still current although issued in 1975, states that the Government is aware that signs can cause problems to the local environment. It also stresses the potential for mounting signs on walls and lampposts to reduce the need for additional posts.

Many uncapped eight foot high grey poles block the pavement for the sake of tiny placards

Do grey posts planted in the middle of the Knightsbridge pavement really provide the right kind of welcome to the heart of London?

Signs can often be fixed neatly onto buildings

And it includes pleasing drawings to illustrate the fact that signs need not wreck views or clutter a village street, that they can be fixed to walls or bollards. On the basis that London is made up of villages it really is time that borough engineers, or whoever else may be responsible, took this ageing but important circular (Department of the Environment, Roads 7/75) more often into account. It is also time the Department of Transport issued one on the subject of clutter in all built-up areas, bidding councils to be much more sensitive. In the intervening years there has been a major shift of attitude with regard to the importance of environment and urban design. The Department of Transport should take the lead and show that its separation from Environment has not made one iota of difference to the weight it attaches to such issues. Local authorities do read and absorb what Whitehall has to say and regular circulars on urban design and street management would strengthen internal council arguments concerning the importance of care and quality.

Signs do not of course only result from highway legislation or stem from official sources. As well as car parks, organisations of all kinds are constantly pressing for metal fingers to point in their direction. Churches, public monuments, shops, all wish to attract a wider public. On the other hand more signs do not necessarily lead to greater understanding, just simple confusion.

Street advertising and hoardings

Advertising on private forecourts can enliven as well as clutter

Pressure has however been arising in a number of boroughs for permission to place commissioned advertising in the form of posters and even video transmitters on traffic barriers, telephone boxes, lampposts, meters and indeed any object in the public domain or encased in freestanding display units. In some cases applicants promise to provide a number for local information or free seats. Surely it would be far better than such sweeteners – but only if the site is suitable – to charge rent. But councils should be as stringent in their choice of location for any addition to the existing confusion both with regard to the character of the area and the actual position on a particular pavement or pole. Well designed, thoughtfully placed street advertisements might add to the vitality of some street scenes. But the incursion of the approved equivalent of flyposting in, say, Bond Street, St. James or Whitehall or any residential area would almost undoubtedly change the ambience for the worse. And safety could well be a factor. This is a different but related issue to pavement boards, which stand back to back in an upturned V outside individual premises, which already provide local colour and information, such as the content and cost of the dish of the day outside pubs and restaurants. They do not need a licence if that part of the pavement counts as private forecourt. But even there too many do reduce space for people.

Estate agency boards

In some parts of London whole streets seem to be permanently up for sale. Competing estate agents's boards sprout from railings and walls, lie forgotten in forecourts and deter the more discerning house hunter. Basically the boards advertise agents – not the property – and there seems no good reason why companies should benefit from deemed, in other words automatic, advertising consent which now so detracts from London's looks. When home ownership was less common, fewer terraces had been converted into flats and the few estate agents still managed estates as well as selling a little property, boards were much less common. Now more people own their own homes, a high percentage of individuals moves every year, in theory five or more flats may be on sale at one time in one former house and estate agents – in reality property shops – flourish on and off the high street. Abuse abounds with cowboys fixing boards where other agents have been appointed or even on properties which are not for sale. Yet agents are easy to find, they can and do advertise in London-wide and local newspapers and magazines and house buyers and sellers could manage equally well without boards.

The Government is reducing the maximum size of boards to approximately three feet by two feet six inches, will allow deemed consent for only one board per property and insist on its removal once there is legal commitment to a lease or sale. Westminster and Kensington and Chelsea both have special dispensation in selected conservation areas to require planning permission for boards, which they can and are likely to refuse on the grounds of their harmful effect upon the local street scene. In these areas local people and agents have supported the move.

In Hampstead one agent accidentally found that sales did not suffer when a list was mislaid and no boards were put up for a month. The local branch manager decided to stop putting up boards and told the Hampstead and Highgate Express: 'We know that people loathe them and we decided that we wanted to be seen to be doing something nice for the area we all make our living out of. Boards only benefit the agencies because they advertise the company involved and they just become a magnet for other boards.'

The quicker this trend grows the better. In addition councils should be able to respond to local pressure to ban boards from selected areas, where they can give an impression of economic instability as well as spoiling the physical environment and architecture. In the meantime, the provision which allows only one board should be more strictly enforced and magistrates encouraged to increase fines to a level which makes the less respectable elements in the industry think a little harder how they go about an increasingly competitive business. Councils should also be empowered to remove all boards if more than one is posted on a property and retain them at a depot for return only on payment of the real costs of removal and storage.

Good advertising for the estate agents perhaps – but not for the property

Westminster has a board watch hotline for reports about unauthorised boards, an idea which could help other councils know where there are obvious problems of proliferation. And in these days of answering machines, hotlines can continue to record such consumer reports and complaints when the town hall locks up.

Litter bins

In this context the number, location and design all count. Sponsorship and wall fitting are again possibilities.

Letter boxes

The letter box curiously is regarded as an urban ornament instead of an excrescence, perhaps because of its colour, shape, sensible location and helpful purpose.

Telephone kiosks

British Telecom looked for a new image and something more vandal-proof when its operations split off from the Post Office. Out went the red, in came a shape which is easier to clean but which has caused heartache and problems. British Telecom consults the local authority about location but needs no planning permission. It does not even pay a licence fee for space on the public highway, let alone rent. Public telephones lose money. Perhaps more shops, pubs, restaurants and offices should be encouraged to provide them as a customer facility which would reduce their need for pavement locations. They would have to rent the pay-machines but equally they would take any profit, as does British Rail at major London stations.

Salt and grit bins and bottle banks

Location is important. So are design, colour and cleanliness. Since salt and grit bins are used by council employees, who know where to find them, there seems no reason why these should not blend into the background in a colour which does not highlight dirt. So many are so dirty so often.

Bus counters, hydrants and odd metal boxes

There may be nothing anyone can do in the way of relocation unless traffic light controls can be pushed underground. But their owners might like to look after them.

Automatic public conveniences

For cleanliness, security and management reasons, the continental import which now adorns street corners and which can be visited for 10p is a vast improvement on many traditional conveniences on or below ground. But location is important, if only to help people find them. In high pressure areas, the single convenience can cause public inconvenience and grouping, which is quite normal in Paris, is essential.

Do salt and grit bins have to be so obvious – and so dirty?

Unloved plants and planters, but perhaps local shopkeepers could be persuaded to accept responsibility

In many areas, there is the demand and the room to group automatic toilets

Street names

While road signs proliferate, the visiting motorist, even the person on foot, may find it difficult to check their bearing or even find a new address. All too often, the name of the street can be missing, invisible or filthy. That is one sign people really do need and councils should negotiate satisfactory solutions. So far as cleansing is concerned, there may be local people who would be prepared to take on this responsibility, particularly if councils could come up with some quid pro quo. It could be something as simple as an annual party.

Street numbers

These are often absent on long stretches of shop fronts and microscopic or located far from the street on people's front doors. Improvements here would actually cheer up highway engineers as better visibility would help the traffic flow.

Planters, tubs, trees, seats

Do they add or subtract from the existing street scene? Some pavements are too narrow for people, let alone boxed greenery. Some streets are so grand they dwarf tubbed conifers and saplings. And since trees need a lot of water, they can be expensive to maintain, unless local firms or residents are prepared to accept responsibility. Also street furniture needs maintenance and renewal. London boasts too many unkempt, often unused or weed-filled concrete boxes dating from the architecturally unloved 1960s. This heritage is disposable.

CONCLUSION

Such joint working parties will naturally find problems in doing the first few streets because of the need for policy decisions, public meetings and negotiations with Whitehall and property owners. But formulae and shortcuts are bound to emerge to speed the process. Although it may take several years to tackle the worst excesses of proliferation or lack of thought, the great thing is to start.

Another case for a wash and brush-up. It does help if the street names are legible

4 Street facelifts

The city is but a framework for living, people messy and perfection impossible, perhaps not even desirable. But if London authorities and Londoners tackled and removed the worst of the dross – litter, scruff and clutter – the subsequent improvement would be something which all could enjoy. It would also contribute to the retention of investment and jobs, help justify the high cost of living and property for residents and create a better ambience for visitors from home and overseas. But a new look for London should not simply stop with a radical spring-clean. There are other aspects of urban management and promotion which, if carried out with style, energy and zeal, would greatly add to the city's quality of life.

ENVIRONMENTAL AUDITS

The removal of clutter is after all only the beginning of an environmental audit, which in the ideal world should move on to more positive action in both residential and commercial areas, taking a closer look at the problem and potential of individual roads and districts, including the impact of traffic, seeing what can be done and who might be able to help.

ROLLING PROGRAMMES

Since the capital is composed of networks of villages developed at different periods of time with very different and constantly evolving traditions, roles, people, architecture and ambience, there obviously can be no universal environmental solution or design panacea. Nor can more than small areas within the 620 square miles of London be tackled at any one time. But even within existing constraints on public expenditure, it is possible to stretch relatively small sums and take advantage of pressures for development and refurbishment to improve the local scene. In addition examples of improvement can create their own momentum and pressure for further action with individuals, companies and groups multiplying the rate of change. The important thing is to create rolling programmes which harness London's massive resources of imagination, time, effort and cash. The majority will be local. Some may have a wider impact. But once an idea is born, the first step must be taken, then the next and the next, so that people can begin to see the impact of change.

In 1985/86 in London 11.2 per cent of net borough expenditure was devoted to general environmental enhancement. This figure compared with 12.1 per cent in the metropolitan districts, that is the big cities outside the capital, and 16.9 per cent in the English shire councils. While certain more deprived areas have of course benefited from urban programme improvements, which are largely funded by government, there is sufficient difference to raise questions about priorities. Many people would consider that the capital was in greater need than rural and semi-rural England.

A fountain in the City enhances the local quality of life

Some boroughs, Camden and Sutton for example, have environmental budgets which over the years achieve substantial improvements through the expenditure of quite small sums on individual works. The consistent spending of say £200,000 a year over five years really can begin to show results if there is a coherent programme. But of course if a local authority, like Westminster, decides to concentrate on upgrading the quality of life for four years with a substantial budget of £3,000,000 allocated for capital works in the first year and £1,750,000 on revenue, plus numerous sponsorship efforts to try to attract money from the private sector, then the impact is obviously immediately greater. The programme spans management as well as physical works and has included the introduction of zone improvement patrols to deal with litter, dog fouling, graffiti, flyposting, estate agency boards and skips; faster permanent repaving to remove unsightly temporary works; improved lighting on housing estates; bridge painting; landscaped traffic islands; sculpture and fountains (such as the young dancer opposite the Royal Opera House and a fountain in Carlos Place); street furniture including the design of new market stalls; and the running costs of floodlighting additional churches. The council is also seeking sponsorship for the cleaning up of street signs, local facelifts such as subways and additional bridge painting. And it is working on a number of area improvements such as Leicester Square, Soho and Oxford Street.

SHARING THE COSTS

These days the pressure for change often stems from local people in particular districts and any subsequent joint programme takes their priorities and willingness to contribute to the cost very much into account. In Richmond for example King

Street traders had been complaining about the environment – it is a major road lined with shops – so the council agreed to carry out highway improvements and provide new street furniture if the shops did up their frontages. Everyone pitched in – the local chamber of commerce, the planning department, councillors and the Richmond Society. It was the council's job to commission the overall contractor with the shops each paying their share of the bill.

BREAKING THE STYLE MOULD

Bromley allocates £50,000 per annum to each of six main shopping centres and holds annual meetings in each area to discuss different improvement possibilities. With an annual rolling programme, this approach means that virtually every high street will be transformed within five to six years. Already the Market Square has been given an attractive facelift with the introduction of a new street livery and better designed guard rails. Instead of uniform grey for posts, traffic lights and the backs of road signs, which is the colour laid down by central government, all such metal objects, plus litter bins, are clad in an unobtrusive elegant green. The same is true of the guard rails which, instead of resembling barricades for controlling obstreperous crowds, have been designed like those on many a British promenade with two simple horizontal rails and are a remarkable improvement on the current urban highway norm. They still separate people on foot from the traffic, but they make the place look friendlier and more relaxed. The council also thought that Market Square deserved something more exciting than London Regional Transport's identikit bus shelter. As a result there is a shelter with a curved roof – and incidentally a relevant mural on a formerly blank wall.

None of these changes would have occurred without imagination and tenacity – imagination to conceive alternatives, tenacity to overcome conservatism and red tape. At one time, traffic posts were painted in black and white stripes. Then the central transport directive opted for grey, on the basis that it would merge into all scenes and not distract drivers. Black is now coming back as an alternative. But if councils wish to use any other colour, they have to apply to the Department of Transport for special permission including the precise shade. And permission has to be given for each particular location where any change is proposed, even if the same colour has been chosen for five areas. This really would seem to be a case of control for control's sake.

Instead of corrals, guard rails in Bromley resemble those on many British seaside promenades

Traffic paint

Bromley has installed a bus shelter to its own design in the local dark green livery in Market Square – and commissioned a mural about H. G. Wells, a local man who made his mark

Bus shelters

The London Docklands Development Corporation has also broken with the bus shelter stereotype and erected a design with a curved roof on the Isle of Dogs. At the moment however such innovation has to be done at someone else's expense. As far as LRT and its associated company are concerned, shelters (and advertising income) seem to be bought off the peg regardless of the sensitivity of different environments. Like British Telecom they virtually do what they like, needing neither planning permission nor to pay for the right to occupy space on the public highway. They do of course need permission for any advertising and have been known to barter the provision of additional shelters against an agreed number with advertisements – and then apply piecemeal for advertisements on some of the ones which were originally meant to be clear. But given the potential income from advertising and the public highway ownership, in some areas it might well be worthwhile for councils to take over the responsibility for providing the shelters and keep the income – or rent the footpath space on more commercial terms.

Guard rails

Again guard rails do not have to be so ugly and inhibiting. Bromley has shown pioneering work in this respect, as has Kingston which has also installed less forbidding railings in its town centre, while Westminster instigated railings topped with gold-painted balls opposite Horseguards Parade. In a more design conscious age, it is simply a question of imagination, not accepting the norm from the pattern book and persuading the engineer that the change will be safe. If simply is the wrong word for upsetting well entrenched ideas, the discussion still needs to start and the tide for change will surely gather strength.

Westminster needed government permission to top the guard rails in Whitehall with glittering gold balls

An even simpler design – with only one horizontal bar – in Kingston

Street maps

It could be helpful too if London offered its citizens as well as visitors properly sited local maps designed to include the most obvious star destinations in each area as well as public facilities such as car parking, libraries, the police, telephone kiosks and conveniences. Lambeth already usefully provides maps in selected locations showing the latter. But unlike many cities there is no systematic provision to help people find out where they are and where to go. London Underground theoretically provides maps at every station between ticket barrier and exits but in practice some are missing. While these should be replaced, they would, in any event, be more useful outside each station instead of within. Local councils also might consider erecting well designed free-standing display units for maps in suitable spaces and places. Even in a period of tight control, they might find the cost worthwhile in building up a more attractive image for their areas. In any event the exercise could be self-financing through the attraction of advertising on the reverse side. Or they might find local sponsors, for example stores, with civic generosity duly and neatly acknowledged.

Overall image

Style and presentation are increasingly important. With the growth of competition in the retail sector and the wish to keep customers on site for as many hours as possible, even stolid surveyors now talk about the theatre of shopping and people's leisure needs. Traders too are prepared to do much more to improve and promote areas as they realise that people are prepared to travel considerable distances and can choose where they spend a day out and shop. Convenience (normally parking and good transport), comfort (ideally pedestrianisation) and ambience are as necessary as plentiful choice of goods to compete with new central speciality and regional centres.

PUBLIC/PRIVATE COOPERATION

A number of areas are beginning to appreciate the need for cooperation between the public and private sectors as a precursor to change. Lewisham set up a special forum with business and other local organisations including LRT, British Rail, the police and unions to consider proposals for the improvement of its town centre. Kensington included local residents and business interests in the forum which led in 1986 to the publication of the Kensington High Street draft action plan. Many of its conclusions and even the principles behind the 46 action points would apply to other centres which straddle busy roads. In design terms, according to the report,

Kensington High Street needed a sense of place with points of interest at which to stop and rest. There was a chance to provide imaginative and interesting shop fronts. Many fine buildings were not noticed or enjoyed for lack of maintenance, the domination of garish shop fronts or because their more interesting features had not been exploited and picked out with paint. Footway services and street furniture could be improved. Cycle racks were needed. Following publication the high street association contributed 50 per cent towards the cost of a shopper's survey and commissioned its own team of designers, a constructive approach which will hopefully be emulated elsewhere.

LESSONS FROM COVENT GARDEN

High streets basically require a regular injection of energy, ideas, action and cash plus continuing imaginative management and promotion. The refurbishment of the The Market, Covent Garden as a speciality shopping area demonstrated a number of ideas which could also be repeated elsewhere.

While a number of indoor shopping centres offer places where people can sit all the year round and watch the world go by, The Market offers a different kind of airy unclaustrophobic ambience away from wind and rain. People can wander in comfort without losing contact with the weather outside. They can enjoy food and drink in this semi outdoors, even in winter – although temporary heaters would sometimes not come amiss. The Market is in one ownership and has a manager. It is swept all day long and litter bins are constantly cleared.

There is of course nothing new in this – after all, London has numerous enclosed shopping centre developments which are kept clean and tidy. The difference in Covent Garden has been the involvement of management in setting a different, almost theatrical scene. The introduction of apple carts has given small businesses the opportunity to sell carefully vetted crafts on one or more days a week for minimal overheads. They add vitality and variety to the atmosphere – and provide a useful money spinner. Management has also been involved in the organisation of events, who have been selected with equal care.

At London Bridge City, a high-level roof was built over the former dry dock to provide a new place for people

49

Theatre of shopping

People enjoy the sense of being in an urban theatre, where they can watch the crowd scenes from the sidelines of a restaurant or cafe or join the throng and temporarily play parts themselves.

High-level shelter

For such a scenario it helps to have good weather or high-level shelter which ideally allows visual communication with the mainstream of London, i.e. it still feels part of the city. Arcades are traditional. But the grander-scale environment has already spread to Hays Galleria in London Bridge City, where a former small Thames dock has been roofed over at high level to provide another such special space. Further west proposals have been considered for covering the South Bank concert halls and art gallery to provide a sheltered area for shopping and a new sense of place. At Portobello Green a tent structure provides shelter over stalls. Elsewhere there has been talk of creating high-level protection over a high street. Architect Derek Latham has designed one in Leeds – a simple pitched glazed roof spanning a 390 foot stretch of Queen Victoria Street and overlapping the existing Edwardian buildings. To open at Christmas 1989, the newly covered street, which is already pedestrian, will remain a street, rather than become an indoor mall.

Apart from the exceptional place where roofing over is possible, it would add greatly to the street scene in many areas if cafes, pubs and restaurants, which provide tables and chairs out of doors in the summer, could add temporary glass-sided structures and awnings with heating in winter so that people could continue to see and be seen all the year round, as is the case on the continent. Some pavements are wide enough, some streets pedestrianised and such a change would bring extra life and sparkle to the darker months.

Design overview

The appointment of an urban designer, particularly in a high street, can create coherence and character which improve the environment for all and should be justified on commercial grounds. It is odd that individual shops will often hire designers to recast fixtures and fittings every five years while the street outside is lucky to have the odd flower basket or litter bin. Urban design, which rates its own institute in the United States, can do so much more. Not only can urban designers explore the use of space but they can be involved in, for example: the selection of a local livery and basic street furniture; the production of shopfront guidelines, not with the intention of imposing anaemic good taste but of ensuring they fit in with existing architectural features; well-designed display units with local maps to show

Signing contributes to the local ambience in docklands and at the South Bank

the location of different shops; good signing, for example, as at South Bank, with a number of fingers pointing to local facilities; imaginative lighting of buildings and the street including the quality of the light itself as well as source and location; the introduction of planting, fountains, statues, sculpture, murals and banners (perhaps the result of an annual competition for art students); well-located, well designed advertisement panels or even some form of larger computerised information and advertising screen on otherwise bleak or windowless walls, especially car parks; an agreed style and system of awnings – they do not have all to be the same colour – so that more shoppers can remain in the dry. (This is an area which is well covered by Gordon Michell in his Royal Fine Art Commission book, Design in the High Street, published by the Architectural Press in 1986.)

Town managers

Unlike indoor shopping centres or department stores, streets and town centres may not be in one ownership but they could well benefit from the appointment of a manager to look after common facilities and services, such as cleanliness and security, and deal with promotion and events. Such a person could help fill unlet units and ensure that any empty shops at least have some form of window display to stem

Banners and flags add colour and vitality to shopping centres

the canker of dereliction and voids. In addition windows can be kept lit late into the night both to attract potential custom and help keep the area alive and safe. In Downtown Denver traders, who came together and arranged joint cleansing and security, were subsequently granted a reduction in property tax payments to city hall.

Even individual residential streets can club together to achieve facelifts contributing, for example, as did local people in one part of Kensington, to the cost of more attractive lampposts than were otherwise on offer.

SMALL PARADES

Of course there are many areas which have more basic problems – small parades, dying high streets or shopping alongside London's key arterial routes. But again there can sometimes be scope for cooperative action. For example, Croydon, as part of its campaign to keep the borough the natural choice, set up the Upper Norwood Improvement Team in 1985 to arrest potential deterioration and, if possible, pump prime local property improvement. UNIT's chairman has been the Speaker of the House of Commons, which adds a certain kudos. But if such exalted leadership is scarcely possible for every neighbourhood shopping parade, let alone proposal for improving the look of London, their choice emphasises the importance of this operation, enlarges its chances of success and provides a message about the need for leadership elsewhere. Other members include local residents, businesses, councillors and officers. Their approach is conventional: for example the use of attractive brick paving, trees and flowers, new street furniture and signs and the provision of brackets to all street lighting so that traders at their request can provide and maintain flower baskets. Other possibilities include landscaped advertising hoardings and cleaning the brick library.

In Tower Hamlets, which has the benefit of urban programme money to help offset its very different history and level of prosperity, the council has been helping shops upgrade their property with grants of 50 per cent of the cost up to a maximum of £1000. Because this individual approach has lacked impact, the borough decided instead to pick a parade, appoint an architect to draw up an improvement scheme and then pay half the cost provided shopkeepers contribute the rest.

Absentee landlords

There is a problem in some areas where parades are owned by institutions or organisations as part of a much larger portfolio and therefore where vacancies or even a rundown appearance will not necessarily rank very high in their order of priority for action. While absentee landlords tend to create local problems, it could help if such landlords used local as well as national agents to help fill vacancies and if details of ownership were to become more widely known. Local people, including the council and the media can help make owners, who may well be institutional, aware that they expect a higher level of interest, better management and maintenance.

Empty property

In some streets however there is no immediate future for shopping and, given the change in shopping patterns and habits, councils may find it sensible in side streets to allow for change of use to different forms of business premises or housing. And of course there could equally be scope on less attractive housing estates, as has been tried on the continent, to allow the change of use of some frequently vandalised flats to small business, offices, even schools. This may theoretically reduce the numbers of homes but helps rebuild a more traditional community with people about at different times of the day.

So far as the longstanding problem of upper floors is concerned, many owners may now find it profitable to arrange independent access and convert for letting on shorthold leases or selling on long lease. As an alternative, Hounslow launched a scheme to lease vacant flats for one to five years at an agreed rent and then let them to homeless families. The scheme has been successful in producing vacant property but more houses than flats and only one above a shop. Some have been turned down because of their poor condition of repair. The council carries out all necessary repairs and guarantees to return the house or flat at the agreed date. Housing associations might also consider similar experiments.

Anglicised strips

London's arterial and radial routes are totally different. Often wide in themselves with wide grass verges and pavements, they provide an opportunity for casual drive-in shops or restaurants in an Anglicised version of the American strip. Many, like

the Romford Road, already have retail warehouses and car showrooms which
forcefully advertise their presence with best buys, flags and bright lights. They are
convenient, zany, lively, a bit raw and fit with the basically fast-moving traffic
environment. The same is true of some 1930s junctions which have shops set well
back circling the crossroads and have room to create drive-in, immediate pick-up
facilities for goods in an area where the demands of traffic have already won the
day.

URBAN DESIGN COMPETITIONS

Finally there is the question of prizes for people who smarten up streets or areas.
Kensington and Chelsea has found it pays to run an annual environmental award
scheme complete with local publicity and pottery plaques to attach to the winning
developments. But as well as local competitions, more attention might be focused
on the possibilities for improvement if there was a major Londonwide annual
competition in the field or urban design and environmental improvement. London

Electricity has organised its brightening up London awards for a second time but, even if these become an annual feature, their scope is much wider than the look of London including, in 1988 for example, categories of people who have contributed to the enjoyment of the young, old, disabled and unemployed as well as the environment per se. A more narrowly focused event could provoke more regular press coverage and so help spread knowledge and interest in different concepts, techniques and products. At the moment, there is all too little interest. There is no trade association, the Design Council has dropped the manual it used to produce on street furniture every five years and there is very little regular information about ideas and best practice even in the associated professional and technical press.

5   Priority for people

Most people, when they are on foot, find car drivers a menace. Most people, when they are at the wheel of a car, act like petty tyrants, speeding away from traffic lights and psychologically scraping the mere mortal who has yet to reach the official haven of the pavement. They roar through puddles, careless of splash and generally behave like well-armed bullies.

Yet traffic, or rather the movement of people and goods, provides the life blood of the city as individuals go to and from work or meetings, shopping, visiting friends and relations, entertainment and other forms of leisure. From the viewpoint of the busy street it can be difficult to grasp the essential quality of this constant flow. However some idea of the relative importance of London's arteries, the North Circular and the M25 as well as the main radials and cross routes, is immediately apparent to any air passenger who looks down at the moving streams or the pattern of lights at night as a plane comes into land.

If some streets provide obvious key lines of communication, where vehicular traffic should have priority (if with regard to people's safety) there are others, sometimes on their own, sometimes in groups which lie to one side, where people live, shop or work and in which there really should be priority for people on foot or cycle. Over the years, since the first experiments in Islington's Barnsbury, the number of environmental areas has increased, as have the number of pedestrian streets or zones. But London is far behind the rest of the country, even further behind some places on mainland Europe, in the creation of havens where motor cars are not necessarily banned – in many streets this is neither possible nor desirable – but where they move under some sufferance and where legally people, not wheeled objects, have and are seen to have the upper hand, or rather foot.

A number of London boroughs have tackled or are taking steps to address this problem with some skill and imagination within existing budgets and the present framework of legislation. But this piecemeal approach, while building up over time, has yet to achieve the sort of impact which will make drivers appreciate they share the public highway and that in cities the official 30mph speed limit does not give them any automatic right to accelerate to that level.

First some schemes and ideas which have made a real difference to parts of London and could be repeated elsewhere:

SPEED HUMPS OR SLEEPING POLICEMEN

Still difficult to negotiate through the bureaucracy, speed humps or sleeping policemen are now possible and have been introduced for example in Kensington and Chelsea and Wandsworth. The emergency services do not like them, bus routes will not have them but they do slow down cars which would otherwise zip down side streets.

THROTTLE OR CHOKE

Hammersmith and Fulham and Tower Hamlets are but two boroughs where some roads have been narrowed by a central island and posts so that vehicles have to slow down for self protection.

A throttle in Fulham forces drivers to slow down and concentrate

Blips

The enlargement of pavements at junctions has a number of advantages. Most accidents take place within 60 feet of corners and the provision of a bulge, which narrows the street exit and entrance and stretches a short distance into the side street, can effectively prevent parking, the major cause of trouble. They also shorten the actual road crossing for people on foot and force motorists – in single file – to slow down to turn the corner more sharply. Camden and Kingston have found this effective.

Central strips

The insertion of a central strip again at the junction of a side road achieves much the same effect, preventing parking through the reduction in road space. It also provides a brief refuge for pedestrians. Kingston has also tried this approach with some success.

In Kingston the installation of a central strip prevents parking near a road junction, helps pedestrians to cross and lowers traffic speed

Narrowed streets, widened pavements

Two south London examples of improvements in high streets with pavements widened and traffic squeezed back into two lanes (Sutton and Kingston)

As part of its urban improvements programme Sutton has been systematically reducing the width of streets for traffic, enlarging pavements and insetting parking bays. The spaces are often separated by trees planted, not in the pavement but in the street, where services are fewer and they have a better chance of survival.

Chicane

The same borough has already adopted a similar principle to improve shopping conditions in heavily trafficked main roads and so reversed the long tradition of widening. The council has taken two lanes away from vehicles, for example at Woodcote Road, Wallington and given them back as footpaths to shoppers and other people on foot with a number of bays left for delivery and bus stops. The introduction of the chicane helps to slow traffic down as it passes through a heavily peopled area. Easier to achieve than full pedestrianisation, which involves all the complexity of road closure, there are many traditional high streets which could benefit from this treatment. In many areas at the moment where there are four traffic lanes, the two outside lanes are almost permanently and often illegally occupied with stationary vehicles. With the Sutton approach, the loss of the outside lanes to moving traffic is accepted on a permanent basis.

SHARED SURFACE

Also in Sutton the High Street, a one-way road, which is shared with pedestrians, has been reduced to three metres. Cars are banned on Saturdays between 10am and 4pm with daily closure proposed. Footpath and road space are level, paved and planted which, together with bollards, indicate the shared surface.

Neal Street, Covent Garden provides a different example. The Camden section of this street is shared all day between people on foot and vehicles with wooden posts or bollards defining the edge of common territory. The paving again is flush from one side of the street to the other. The posts also indent into the pedestrian walkway to create parking bays for deliveries. While there is no ban on cars, the overall design and narrowing of the street effectively make drivers take care and slow down. In Westminster, just across the borough boundary, the same street is pedestrian with deliveries only allowed up to a fixed hour. There are a number of other similar schemes in central London including South Molton and Gerrard Streets. Such improvements do not cost a great deal and if more boroughs were to draw up systematic programmes, people would feel there really were areas in which they were comfortable and the car no longer king.

TEMPORARY ROAD CLOSURE

There are already examples – Sutton High Street and a number of markets on their busiest days. It would be a good idea to explore the potential for using this system on a more flexible basis in other areas. For example, sections of Charlotte Street might be closed on Saturday nights, or even more frequently, for three months in the summer to allow restaurants (with licences) to spread, not just onto the footpath, but onto the road as well.

In Oxford or Bond Streets, it might be possible to close off several blocks during the Christmas rush and the first week of the sales. Excluded traffic would temporarily have to be diverted but crossing routes would remain open. This approach has been adopted on a permanent basis on one of Ottawa's main shopping streets and there has recently been a complete refurbishment of street furnishings, cafes and kiosks to compete with the draw of a new downtown shopping centre. If this was to happen in London Westminster could, for such busy festive times, encourage and temporarily licence speciality food kiosks, a limited amount of fair equipment and entertainments. On much the same principle, the Government might consider licensing a summer season outdoor cafe in Trafalgar Square.

Total pedestrianisation is not essential to improve the shopping or any other environment. Vehicles can be restricted to certain times of day or careful design of the shared street surface can give pedestrians priority. The Westminster/Camden border in Neal Street (left), Kingston town centre (above) and Sutton High Street (right)

Subways

Bare of ornament, ill-lit and lonely, subways are rarely places for people even if they do have priority. But what sort of person or society condemns the unprotected pedestrian to descend into the potential abyss, while people in vehicles enjoy the light and relative safety of the earth's surface it is hardly surprising that individuals frequently risk the traffic snarl. To avoid the dismal and even more dangerous detour underground. In any shift to people priority, pedestrians should more regularly have their own street crossing time included in the programming of traffic lights, and long enough to allow for the lame or elderly as well as joggers and keep fit fanatics. Or by law they should have right of way over turning vehicles. Where subways are considered essential, they need first-class lighting and controlled circuit television to reduce the sense of isolation and increase security. Many subways could do with a more substantial facelift bringing in the professional designer and perhaps the psychologist to improve links with the city above, upgrade the environment and limit opportunities for damage and physical attack. On the continent some subways, for example in Paris and Munich, have been created on a sufficiently large scale to allow for shops and cafes, which attract people and therefore become more or less self-policing.

Parking Control

Hounslow has not merely opted for residents parking but drawn up an ingenious scheme for tackling the problem of commuters who leave their cars in side streets and continue their journeys by public transport. In Chiswick the council is banning parking for one hour a day, for example from noon to 1pm in one street and 1pm to 2pm in another, and sending in traffic wardens at those times to ticket offending vehicles. Residents can use separate parking bays all day.

The readoption of roads by owners of local property is a more extreme solution taken by one street in Chelsea, in which residents found their life made misery by the habitués of a local public house who double parked and generally caused chaos. Every ratepayer in the cul-de-sac agreed to the change, which meant rates were reduced. Now they all club together to pay the council to provide on contract the services they have foregone, such as highway maintenance and street lights.

Responsibility for parking and enforcement should be given a total overhaul. At the moment responsibility is split for different offences between the police, traffic wardens and local authorities. Some London boroughs pay traffic wardens and then receive the charge for excess time – but not the benefit of fixed penalties for illegal overtime. The Home Office looks after the police who normally have more important duties on their mind than traffic. Local authorities work to the Department of the Environment and traffic regulation comes under the Department of Transport. Councils have pressed for total responsibility so that control of illegal parking could become more like building, litter, planning and health enforcement. In Washington DC, which formerly dealt with parking in much the same way as London, parking has been handed to the local authority whose staff are linked by radio to central control and the headquarters computer. With power to issue fixed penalty tickets and/or clamp wheels, they can check whether owners of vehicles have any outstanding unpaid parking tickets. If they have, then clamps are not released until all other fines have been paid as well. In the first year, the system made a profit.

PEDESTRIAN PRIORITY

However it is possible to go further in giving people priority. In the early 1980s Leicester wanted to introduce a new legal status for pedestrians within selected areas of the inner city. In mainland Europe, in particular the Dutch *woonerf* (living yard), environmental areas can be reinforced by laws under which vehicles legally give way to people on foot or cycle just as at sea steam gives way to sail. The Midlands city planned to include a clause to this effect in the Leicestershire Act but was opposed by Whitehall on the grounds that physical changes such as ramps, narrowed streets and changes of paving colour to outline parking bays, could be done under existing legislation. It was also pointed out that, while drivers were likely to react to physical road alterations, they were unlikely to give way to pedestrian superiority simply in the name of the law. Since action was their prime consideration, Leicester did not argue the toss. However the scheme cost about £2,250 for each of the 80 houses and, although values as well as the local quality of life in Worthington Street may have been enhanced, to apply similar treatment all over Leicester, let alone London, would be very expensive indeed. Yet if Britain had some form of legislation to enable the declaration of areas of pedestrian priority within fixed boundaries without elaborate physical work, progress could be made that much more quickly. Such a law could also help clarify rights of way. And the introduction of more flexibility in urban speed limits – for example 20mph for most residential areas, 10mph in crowded shopping streets – could be an additional bonus.

6 Space in the city

If a large number of London's streets are improved in terms of appearance, comfort and convenience, the capital will immediately benefit. Improvements will range from the relatively quiet backwater to the revitalised local high street with its busyness, excitement and fun. Such streets may not be open space in the traditional sense but they are open, provide space and, upgraded, could greatly add to the quality of city life. They can also link up with the existing network of squares, parks, heath, woodland and any additional small oases, green or otherwise.

MAJOR NEW OPEN SPACE

But while most of London has reasonable or good access, some parts of the capital are less well endowed and the insertion of green areas as an essential part of new infrastructure could help attract property and other investment. There is a shortage of maps showing a bird's eye view of the capital but the London Topographical Society's satellite photograph immediately highlights the virtually unrelieved density of the urban environment in inner east London on both sides of the Thames. New towns in Britain and overseas have shown the importance of the physical environment in setting the framework and the same principles hold for the regeneration of the older city. The use of section 52 agreements for the creation and management of new open space may be one possibility. Another could be the setting up of a joint public/private company with local land owners and developers, which can borrow money for building planned landscape infrastructure on the presumption of subsequent increases in land values. The London Docklands Development Corporation used this method successfully in the Greenland Dock.

The 'urban green', as it was called by the 1984 The Green Cities Congress, should enhance people's lives by providing space for leisure, sport, art, culture, relaxation and peace; making cities more beautiful; producing food and fuel; and involving people in its creation and maintenance.

EXISTING OPEN SPACE

Since opportunities have to be seized within the existing framework, it is worth emphasising the scope and potential of London's present open space. Apart from streets, and these are an important asset in this respect, many homes have gardens. Then there are pocket parks, fields, squares, communal residents's gardens (for example in Kensington), public open space in housing estates, school grounds, playing fields, tennis clubs and centres, cleared open space and meadows, garden centres, allotments, churchyards, cemeteries, city farms, ecological wilderness and waste land, not forgetting of course the grander parks, royal or metropolitan, woods, heath and London's system of rivers, canals and reservoirs.

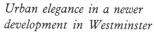

Even without a restaurant, churchyards provide oases of open space in the city

Urban elegance in a newer development in Westminster

SOME LONDON INITIATIVES

A great deal of activity and improvement is already happening, often taking advantage of the energy of people and in some cases additional sources of cash such as the Government's urban programme. Here are a few ideas which could well be useful in other parts of the city.

LOCAL INVOLVEMENT

School competition

Bromley involved a local primary school in producing ideas through essays and drawings for a former bus turning area. An exhibition was held, the local paper published pictures (of the children as well), the area now has its own village green with cast iron instead of concrete lampposts and the residents have provided and now manage flower baskets. Because local people have been involved, they have accepted responsibility.

Community management

Southwark introduced its Facelift scheme, in part funded through the urban programme. Groups suggesting suitable sites for treatment normally have to be prepared to put in work clearing and on subsequent maintenance and management, for example cleaning up litter and locking and unlocking gates. Brent has also involved local people in the creation and management of new open space helping with the original planting and painting and now maintaining shrubs, locking and unlocking and generally tidying up.

Local involvement appears also to limit vandalism. In the course of transformation of one open space in Southwark into an ecological garden, the tools used each Monday morning to turn up in the pond. When the young culprits were caught and shown around, they became sufficiently interested to help dig the butterfly garden and signed their names on the walls as helpers. There were no further problems. The borough has published examples in a booklet called Brightening up your Neighbourhood, The Story of the Southwark Environment Programme. It contains a Facelift application form (Freepost) with space for details about potential projects including their location, ownership of land, possible benefits to the local area, the amount of work the group will be able to carry out, the sort of help required from the council, such as money, materials, technical advice and the work itself, and the ability for after-care. The booklet does however hint that there can be problems when the initial enthusiasts move away.

Organisation umbrella

Sutton launched the Sutton Conservation Group as an umbrella organisation for volunteer groups such as the London Wildlife Trust, the Surrey Wildlife Trust and the British Trust for Conservation Volunteers to help manage and conserve local green space. In so doing it has discovered an enormous human resource. More than 350 people attended the initial meeting in April 1987 and a programme of some 120 events were organised for anyone who wished to spend an hour or a day planting trees, digging ponds, building paths or creating wildlife gardens. The first event attracted more than 80 people who built more than 100 bird and bat boxes. About 130 people from a dozen local organisations helped clean up the Wandle River one Sunday. And in one year volunteers planted more than 4000 trees. The council provides transport, when necessary, tools, insurance and technical guidance.

Adopt-a-plot

Sutton has also worked up an adopt-a-plot policy with management agreements drawn up between the council and a number of trusts – the London Wildlife Trust has taken on Wilderness Island and Surrey Wildlife Trust an oak wood, hedgerow and wildflower meadow in a formerly formal park. The general approach of the council in providing a framework for action and encouraging local people and groups, it could be a school, to take on the responsibility of looking after particular areas is obviously a good idea.

London enthusiasts

Voluntary effort, goodwill and seed money is available on a scale which crosses borough borders. Set up in 1981, the London Wildlife Trust manages about 40 sites throughout the capital and generally identifies suitable sites and works for their protection. The British Trust for Conservation Volunteers has more than 30 local groups in the region, which play their part in the creation and maintenance of open space and again provide fellowship in the shared experience of creative effort. BTCV is one of the founding members of UK 2000, the organisation sponsored by government to bring together voluntary bodies, industry and government for environmental improvement and economic regeneration. The other founder members were the Civic Trust, Community Service Volunteers, the Groundwork Foundation, the Keep Britain Tidy group, the Royal Society for Nature Conservation, Friends of the Earth and the Prince of Wales Committee. The organisation has its own funds and is prepared to contribute towards feasibility studies or pay for project leaders for work done by other suitable bodies. However while it provides an additional spur to improvement and change and will obviously contribute to London as well as the rest of the country, the needs of London should not be swallowed into a national organisation of this kind. London needs its own capital improvement campaign.

WILDLIFE AND ECOLOGY

Wildlife and ecology are very much the modern idiom, not simply as part of the growing green ethos but also because such open spaces need little maintenance. Meadows only need occasional cutting and wood plantations present fewer problems, including vandalism, than lollipop trees.

LEFTOVER LAND

Brent is transforming land which many people might simply not notice, let alone use – for example, a steep railway embankment as a children's playground with slide and a major roundabout (now linked by footbridge) as a new wildlife garden. The same borough is working on plans for a rolling programme to improve school playgrounds from the traditional squares of grey tarmac or grass to include ponds and wildlife.

In Brent a railway embankment has been transformed into a children's playground with slides fixed to the slope

A PERMANENT GARDENS EXHIBITION

In the days when there was a borough lottery, Barnet designed five scented gardens in existing local parks. Such happy innovations are all too rare. Garden festivals have shown that imagination could transform parts of existing parks. Magazines often show the potential of the traditional rectangle which is the London garden. It would be an interesting experiment if one London park could lay out a series of such rectangles as a permanent but evolving exhibition of typical London gardens and patios complete with grass, trees, paths, mounded earth, labelled plants, sculpture, children's corners, barbeque areas, ponds and possibly fountains.

URBAN TRAILS

More or less green city walks and more rural trails have become increasingly popular.

Greenways

In Camden Growth Unlimited has developed the Greenways scheme from Kings Cross to Lincoln's Inn as a pleasant signposted minor trafficked route. As part of the programme, it helped local people to improve their immediate environment and transform derelict sites into new open space, which they then manage. The group has also initiated a window box scheme providing 450 boxes, plants and care leaflets to residents. Funds have come mainly from Camden plus some donations.

Green belt trails

Barnet has made its more rural scene more accessible through new footpaths, bridges and bridleways through woods, former railway land and an overgrown cemetery. MSC labour has been used.

Green Chain

In south London, the Green Chain connects a string of more than 300 public and private open spaces including parks, woods, playing fields, allotments, commons, farmland and golf courses from New Beckenham in Bromley through Lewisham to Greenwich and Bexley, where it links with the river at the barrier and Thamesmead. The 15.5 mile route is signposted and free leaflets on separate sections provide good local maps showing bus stops, places to eat and social, architectural and historic points of interest such as Eltham Palace. A joint project between the boroughs and the Greater London Council, the Green Chain took several years to achieve but at relatively little expenditure through the use of Manpower Services Commission labour.

Canal towpath

In inner London the canal towpath has been almost completely open to the public for some years. The British Waterways Board basically leaves its gradual improvement to local councils, including the provision and emptying of litter bins, while it concentrates its energies on Paddington Basin and Limehouse Basin where there is sufficient land for major developments. Because it owns so little land along the rest of the waterway, the potential for improvement lies very much with other property

Part of the Green Chain in south London, one of the city's more rural urban trails

owners. The GLC set up a consultative committee of the relevant boroughs. Since its abolition, a similar committee has failed, at least initially, to attract all the relevant boroughs, which illustrates the difficulties of achieving joint policies, improvements and even maps which cross borough boundaries.

London Wall Walk

On a totally different scale, the Museum of London in 1984 launched the London Wall Walk to follow, where possible, the line of the old city wall from the Tower to the museum. The route is marked by 21 tiled panels which contain information about the buildings and history of the immediate area and, like a treasure hunt, map the route to the two nearest panels. Thoroughly imaginative in concept, the museum found the whole exercise more difficult than expected. It had to get planning permission for each panel mainly from the City Corporation, but also Tower Hamlets. There was the necessary permission from the Department of the Environment, where its land was involved or for any panels mounted on the wall, which is listed. Then there was the question of sponsorship – at £800 per panel or cost price to the manufacturing company concerned – with letters to local business and more letters to local charities to fill the gap and pay for the design and drawings.

A small guide has been published price £1.50 but, given the regular maps and information, the route is much easier to follow than the pavement arrow studs of the Jubilee Walk.

CAPSULES OF HISTORY

The siting of additonal information panels to buildings could also be used as a back-up to more urban walks, trails or heritage parks. Apart from the trans-London blue plaque system now operated by English Heritage, a number of boroughs have evolved their own systems for providing occasional panels which bring the past into the present and help visitors in particular to avoid the need for constant recourse to the guide book. Examples include Crosby Hall, Chelsea, the Market Square, Bromley and, with very brief information, a number of buildings in the City's square mile. While the traditional blue plaques marking the London properties of the famous are very expensive at more than £700, the metal story sheets used by Bromley work out at about £70 each, less than one-tenth the price. Such brief capsules of history are very usual in North American cities. In Baltimore, for example, they contain

Capsules of history add interest to the city

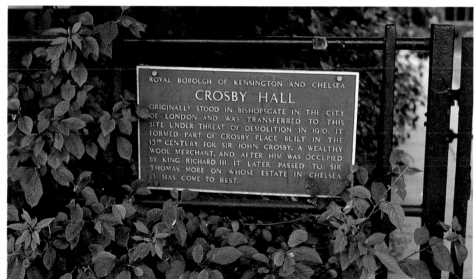

perhaps 150 words about the building and pay homage to the mayor as well as the financial sponsor. A series of small well designed panels – perhaps this is another subject for a competition – could equally enhance the London scene.

These few examples can only begin to give the flavour of current trends with potential for further development. But there is the strong emergence, often within the conservation movement but also among tenants and other local groups, of people willing to create and manage open space. There is also a movement away from the manicured formality of municipal thinking. But where are the pubs in the park? Is all that football really necessary? What about planting fruit trees, not just in green spaces but also along highways, like the apple trees of Solihull – and letting anyone who will enjoy the harvest?

JOINT BOROUGH PROJECTS

Councils can and should, wherever possible, act as local enablers but London, with Government backing, has to find new or better ways of creating linked open space and pedestrian routes which cross borough boundaries. In this context marketing too presents a problem, with far too many borough publications which forget the continuation of facilities and even streets just across the road. Undoubtedly it helps to have one organisation – possibly a trust – in charge, ideally run by a dynamic highly motivated individual who can wear down the natural sloth of the bureaucratic committee cycle and win the support of the private sector. There is the apocryphal tale of the 21-kilometre park under the Vancouver's elevated light railway, which was created in effect by a provincial government minister. She persuaded national governments to donate an international mall of flags, Holland to give one million bulbs, an airline to transport them, a sports firm to create a jogging path, another company to provide lighting and so on until the city found itself with a new park for free. Unless London can enlist the support of someone with similar verve and influence, even with sponsorship and cooperation, public pump-priming is likely to be necessary.

7 The Thames for pleasure

The greatest opportunity for creating a chain of open space and transforming an underused thoroughfare into a place for people lies of course in the Thames. This broad waterway provides the city with its largest open area, not firm beneath the feet, as is the traditional park, but offering a tremendous sense of freedom from the congestion and tension of urban life and a backcloth for individual buildings, bridges, spaces and human activity of grey living water, constantly changing according to tide, wind and weather.

RECAPTURING WATERFRONTS

Once it was the only major highway, not simply for trading ships from all parts of the globe but also for Londoners, grandees in the equivalent of today's chauffeur-driven Rolls Royce or Jaguar and small ferries for lesser mortals, which plied between the two sides to offset the shortage of bridges. Increasingly however it became a working river with many buildings rising vertically from its banks. Industry – including power stations, gas works and factories as well as the docks – gradually dominated the scene, except of course in the most historical areas with their palaces and parks. Its water was increasingly polluted. In more recent times, as has happened all over the world, manufacturing industry closed or moved away from the city centre to more spacious surroundings and links with motorways. In addition traditional inner-city docks and harbours were left to decay as container ships berthed nearer the traffic lanes of the open sea. Such idle derelict land might have had little potential had it not been for the associated improvement in the quality of the water, partly as a result of the disappearance of industry, partly because of growing environmental concern. Nevertheless the availability of central sites combined with cleaner rivers and docks meant that cities in many countries began to explore their former backyards and found it possible and highly rewarding to recapture their waterfronts as exciting places for people.

In spite of the opportunities presented by central government's creation and funding of the London Docklands Development Corporation, London has to date failed to

A Thames authority could look after the quality of the foreshore

achieve this dramatic turnround in perception of the river, its development and use. Of course the conversion of waterside warehouses into upmarket homes has proved successful in commercial and conservation terms. And a number of new blocks of flats have appeared to the greater and lesser enhancement of the riverside scene. But it should have been possible to create much more continuous public access along the edge of this great open space, sometimes through the ground floors of existing and new buildings, as in Chiswick, if not on a deck without, to allow some structures to plant their feet in the water. It should also have been possible to open up more of East London, in particular, to the river, to green or create hard landscaped parklets on more sites in front of new riverside pubs or restaurants as well as the ubiquitous waterfront housing.

The LDDC has of course backed new river bus services, although these have been seen mainly as a new form of commuter travel for people whose home and work are based sufficiently near the growing number of piers.

A NEW NATIONAL PARK

In reality however the Thames is not some simple traffic artery like the Cromwell, Finchley, Tottenham Court and Commercial Roads or even the Embankment, for journeys connected with the pressures of daily life. Like the centre of Covent Garden, many Thameside buildings and open spaces are more suited for time off rather than time on, for play, leisure, relaxation, a holiday or even a holi-morning. Tourism is an increasingly important industry to the capital and many more people from this country as well as abroad will be visiting London. The London Tourist Board's tourism strategy suggests a 30 per cent increase in overseas visitors, or some 2,500,000 more men, women and children, over the next decade. In addition, with the Channel Tunnel and its new terminal at Waterloo scheduled to open in 1993, there is the prospect of more people coming for one or more days from mainland Europe. And these forecasts take no account of British visitors, the majority of whom are likely to enjoy more leisure and higher incomes. Most important of all, for Londoners, and that includes the less advantaged, an enhanced Thamesside could provide the focus for all kinds of free-time activities.

Stretching many miles, the Thames River Park would be a new kind of park for the capital city, not simple green open space with trees, although there would be some, but studded with famous landmarks, museums, centres for entertainment including concerts and plays, simulated experiences, for example through re-creation of periods of the past or life in space, restaurants, pubs and above all places for people, what the Americans call festival markets. Like Covent Garden, these are areas which are fun to visit, provide a sense of participation for all the urban players of the day in the architectural equivalent of an open-air theatre and offer opportunities for impulse purchases including food and drink.

In their proposal for a Battle of Britain monument in the Surrey Docks, Professor Michael Sandle, Theo Crosby and Pedro Guedes of Pentagram Design describe the river as a tourist artery. And that is exactly what it could and should be, although tourist is perhaps the wrong word since the Thames would become the framework for a national, even international, leisure park for residents and visitors alike. On a massive scale, it offers a palette of cultural and other leisure facilities as well as a chance to mingle with the crowd or find riverside solitude and space.

Most of this development is already there and needs only imaginative leadership and organisation to inspire and coordinate existing operators and land owners and provide a marketing framework.

Major Thameside facilities

Currently major Thamesside facilities include:

- Entertainment centres such as:
  Waterman's Arts Centre, Brentford
  Riverside Studios, Hammersmith
  Battersea Park (summer seasons in tent)
  South Bank with the National Theatre, the Royal Festival Hall, the Queen
      Elizabeth Hall and the National Film Theatre and the
  Mermaid.

  Further theatres – the new Players at Charing Cross, County Hall, the Shakespearean Globe and Wilton's Music Hall – are in the planning pipeline.

- Art galleries:
  Tate
  Hayward and the
  Courtauld Collection on its move to Somerset House

- Historic palaces and houses:
Hampton Court
Ham House
Marble Hill
Syon House
Fulham Palace
Crosby Hall
Lambeth Palace
Palace of Westminster (with perhaps a minibus detour to Buckingham Palace)
Banqueting House, Whitehall
Tower of London
Edward III's manor house (remains only) and
Greenwich.

- Some of London's greatest churches:
Westminster Abbey
Southwark Cathedral and at a short distance
St. Paul's Cathedral plus
A host of smaller masterpieces in the City.

- Museum and other visitor attractions:
Living Steam Museum
Florence Nightingale Museum at St. Thomas's Hospital
Museum of the Moving Image, South Bank
Bankside Museum
Legal London
Roman London
Financial London
The Monument
HMS Belfast
London Dungeon
Space Adventure 3001
Tower Bridge
The Cutty Sark
National Maritime Museum
North Woolwich Railway Museum and
Thames Barrier.

Further proposals include the Richmond Museum, Battersea Power Station indoor theme park, an attraction or museum on South Bank, a new London experience at Tower Hill, the Design Museum at Butler's Wharf, the Metropolitan Police Museum at Wapping, the Academy of St. Martin's in the Field, Wapping, a museum of Victorian life at St. Mark's, Silvertown, museums of nineteenth century London and future science plus other ideas in the Royals and possible attractions at Barking Creek.

- Riverside shopping: Major centres at Richmond, Kingston, Putney High Street and Surrey Quays with Canary Wharf, the eastern end of the Royals and Thamesmead as strong possibilities, (not to mention the new M25 regional shopping centre outside London's boundaries at Lakeside, Thurrock at the northern end of the Dartford Tunnel).

Minor centres at Barnes and Wandsworth Bridges and the Tower of London.

Existing and potential speciality shopping centres or festival markets include Chelsea Harbour (with access to the Kings Road), Battersea, South Bank (currently books, music and crafts but proposals for expansion are under consideration and of course there are existing links across the river with the new Villiers Street and on to Covent Garden), a new weekend market nearby at Gabriel's Wharf, Hays Galleria, St. Katharine-by-the-Tower, Tobacco Dock, Butler's Wharf, Port East beside the West India Dock and Brunswick and South Docks. In addition shopping is included in proposals for Westminster Pier.

- Parks:
  Hampton Court
  Richmond
  Kew Gardens
  Syon Park
  Dukes Meadow
  Fulham Palace
  The Hurlingham Club (private)
  Chelsea Physic and Ranelagh Gardens
  Battersea Park
  Island Gardens and
  Greenwich

with stretches of riverside promenade for example at Chiswick, South Bank and London Bridge City. The Countryside Commission has proposed a proper linked riverside walk beside or near the Thames as part of its long distance route from Gloucestershire to the Thames Barrier, of which some 23 miles or 13 per cent will be located in London.

- Yacht havens and mooring facilities:
Brentford
Chelsea Harbour
St. Katharines

plus proposals in docklands

- There are a number of hotels, pubs and restaurants but the Thames in its new role should attract many more.

- Public transport access includes:
London City Airport
Battersea Heliport and
British Rail mainline stations such as Waterloo (the Channel Tunnel terminal), Charing Cross, London Bridge, Blackfriars, Cannon Street and Fenchurch Street

A number of other British Rail stations such as Greenwich and North Woolwich to the east and Richmond, Kew Gardens and Hampton Wick to the west, plus numerous underground and docklands light rail stations including Putney Bridge, Vauxhall, Pimlico, Westminster, Embankment, Waterloo, London Bridge, Tower Hill, Wapping, Limehouse and Island Gardens.

THE OPPORTUNITIES

Sit and stare

It must be possible to add to the numbers of places where it is possible to sit, eat, drink and watch the magic of the moving river and reflections, particularly at night.

County Hall

Whatever else County Hall becomes, the great terrace should provide a popular stage or place for people. This area would link well via the Jubilee Gardens with the proposed shopping/festival market centre associated with the South Bank Centre and new activities including a museum and weekend market in the Coin Street development.

A sculptural building

The temporary car park in front of the Shell Centre provides an opportunity for a structure and activity which reflects the area's festival heritage and again links in with the South Bank Centre. The Géode in Paris, a stainless steel sphere reflecting the passing scene and sky and containing a highly popular Omnimax which shows special high-quality films designed to envelope their audience, gives an imaginative lead. The site has been owned by the London Residuary Board with the South Bank Board receiving the income from its use as a car park to help fund the organisation of special events and the cleaning and security of the local riverside walk. Current development proposals include a theatre and a replacement of the 1951 Skylon.

The site in front of the Shell building presents an opportunity for a sculptural building

Architectural quality

A number of sites, such as the southern end of Vauxhall Bridge, the next phase of London Bridge City, Charing Cross, the South Bank, Woolwich Arsenal, the south side of the Royals and the riverside at Barking, have proposals or are being considered for development which will transform large stretches of Thamesside. It is important that both architecture and activities enhance the river as the capital's newest park. A number of good examples exist already – the new Crown Estate development at Vauxhall Bridge with a small section of riverside walk and London Bridge City with offices, hospital, covered speciality shopping centre, restaurants, its own pier and river walk complete with fountain and follies. Both have captured a scale, interest and excitement lacking in so many of the new pitched roof residential warehouses which are most reminiscent of London's medieval riverside or a present-day Dutch canal.

Garden festival

A derelict site, such as the former Beckton works just east of docklands, could be used for Britain's next international garden festival in the mid 1990s. 'Garden festivals could become a laboratory for our urban future', according to landscape architect Robert Holden in the Architects' Journal, February 4, 1987. Such an approach would produce a very different form of festival from those held in this country to date and could, he believes, contain experiments in defensible space for housing, new forms of office and commercial development, industrial landscapes, experiments in provision and management of urban wildlife and conservation, a new marriage between sculpture and urban life, alternatives to agricultural land use, experiments in urban forestry, new ways of relating landscape and buildings, experiments in derelict land restoration and new forms of parkland and open space.

Floating coaches

Given the number of existing visitor attractions on or near Thamesside, the travel trade should begin to think in terms of floating river coaches and so shift a great deal of the increase in tourist traffic and therefore the growth in numbers of outsize tour buses off London's roads. Visitors may need transport from their hotel to the river – preferably by mini buses – but once there, all kinds of possibilities emerge – not just the traditional trip from Westminster to Greenwich and the barrier or upstream to Hampton Court but tailormade excursions visiting the art galleries or a series of museums or a museum, a palace and a shopping centre. In addition, the more independent should be able to centre their day on the Thames, buy day river passes and find smaller ferries, river buses or water taxis to switch from one attraction to the next. For these journeys, as opposed to commuting to work, it matters much less that boats have to take account of the exigencies of the tide and cannot simply brake as they pull alongside a pier.

NEED FOR SPECIAL ORGANISATION

This transformation of the Thames will not come about by chance. While the riverside may already boast a scattering of precious stones of attractions, it needs organisation, energy and flair to thread them and others into a necklace or pattern of development and management which will make the waterfront a new focus for London.

In the past the Greater London Council administered a Thamesside Consultative Committee which included representatives of the riparian boroughs and water users and considered all major planning applications. It was not very effective, in part because it met too rarely to be sure that comments would reach the relevant local council in time to make any impact. This committee died along with the GLC in 1986 and has been resurrected by the London Planning Advisory Committee. But the riverside boroughs in reality operate in a vacuum only consulting the local authority on the other side and perhaps the Royal Fine Art Commission on developments of potential national importance. However unless there is a public inquiry, all comment can be ignored or result in minor compromise. No one with any authority is really thinking of a creative role for the river, the combined impact of proposals in the riverside scene, or ways in which one development or activity can tie in or help another. There is also no one place to which members of the public can learn about new schemes and ideas or existing attractions and facilities.

The London Tourist Board set up a river group following the publication of its tourism strategy with representatives from Thames Water, the Port of London Authority, which traditionally manages the water, the LDDC and Thames Passenger Services. However it does not include land owners, users, local authorities or London campaigners and perforce its work is focused on the use of the water whereas the role of such a body, except for travel from one side to another and east to west, should relate to activities on the land.

POSSIBLE FRAMEWORKS FOR ACTION

If the Thames is to be handled with the acumen and imagination it deserves to become a new kind of park for the capital city, there are a number of alternative routes, any one of which would be more hopeful and helpful.

Tourist development action plan

1. The English Tourist Board could set up a tourist development action plan aimed at upgrading the environment as well as new marketing.

Urban Commission

2. The Thames could be declared Britain's first urban national park with its own park board and powers comparable to those controlling other national parks. Although the Countryside Commission has instigated proposals for a Thames Walk through London as part of a new long-distance route, a new Urban Commission might provide a more apposite framework for the development and management of the riverside as a whole.

An enjoyable new section of river walk at London Bridge City

Development authority

3. A Thames Development Authority could be created with representatives from public and private sector including major interests, central as well as local government, land owners or operators of key attractions and the London Tourist Board.

THE ROLE

Whatever the organisation, its role would be:
- to promote the Thames and Thamesside
- to activate the use and development of the river and bank so as to improve the quality of life in London life

- to consider carefully the effect of any development on or over the water through the mooring of major vessels or floating buildings in terms of use, effect on services and aesthetics
- to enhance the metropolitan riverside panorama through conservation and the encouragement, possibly by competitions, of new buildings and works of art. (If it was able one day to persuade the Government to demolish the Department of the Environment building in Marsham Street and so restore the view of the Houses of Parliament from Waterloo Bridge, so much the better.)
- to create an urban park of international significance embracing art, history, music, the theatre, education, sport, the market place and open space and allow for oases of solitude as well as people magnets.

Public access to the water's edge would be a major objective with every encouragement to the establishment of a first-class long-distance Thames Path.

The creation of riverside resorts would be another important aim as would be the improvement of hard and soft landscaping of both public and private development through a rolling programme of investment. Its quality would be of the utmost importance bearing in mind the scale of individual projects and their context as seen from the opposite river bank as well as by individuals on the spot. There could be competitions including one for the Greenwich foot tunnel, which underplays its atmospheric role beneath the river.

General management and the staging and coordination of events would be a prime responsibility, ranging for example from cleanliness and security to the floodlighting of buildings and parks, the encouragement of open-air art and artists, the introduction of a giant computerised news and advertisement screen, clusters of banners, Thames fairs and ethnic festivals, laser shows, fireworks and sophisticated son et lumiére. In many respects, the former Bristol Marketing Board, led by private enterprise but involving and backed by the public sector, could be a useful example.

First-class marketing would be essential.

Finally it would require really imaginative leadership to sell the change in perception, inspire existing ringside (or mostly bankside) participants to play an even better part, give the boroughs a lead, encourage outside sponsors and find a host of others to contribute still more ideas.

8 Trees, flowers, colour and art

TREES

The British climate encourages trees, flowers and green grass which grow with ease and abundance to help compensate for the grey sky which all too often looms overhead. When clouds grizzle and local buildings stand in unrelieved stone or concrete, London can present a grim facade, which is a good reason for introducing colour, as blessed by nature or, with sensitivity, man's best artifice.

Trees in particular are a constant reminder to the city dweller of the seasons, as they stand stripped of leaves in late autumn, swell through the winter, then bud, burst into pale green, followed by the heavier tones of summer, and finally the changing shades of autumn before the cycle begins again. In October 1987 when so many great specimens fell after battle with the great wind, they also forced Londoners to appreciate the power of the elements even in a modern sophisticated city.

Information

Trees can of course overshadow, make pavements slippery, as leaves fall on wet pavements, and endanger foundations of property. But generally however they enhance the environment and they make a formidable difference to the quality of life between suburb and inner city.

While planting is popular, with imaginative schemes like the Forest of London, there is a need for more general knowledge about the choice of different trees for different locations, their planting and maintenance. A small fir or bay tree in a tub may look quite well defining the forecourt of a restaurant but ridiculously out of place in a main thoroughfare. The container may also become just one more litter bin and require regular watering, in other words, looking after. Even in the ground, trees may need extra watering during their early life, for which the best solution may be an agreement with local residents or business to achieve the necessary attention. Many local authorities have built up experience with types and nurturing of trees and there could be scope for a London conference to exchange as much technical and practical information as possible.

Window boxes can be almost as prolific as the traditional herbaceous border

Tree preservation orders

It would also be useful if the Government were to review the administration of tree preservation orders in cities. At the moment each order has its own map with full details despatched to individual property owners as well as taking up further space in town hall files. Since councils have to be sensible in consideration of applications for pruning and replacement there could be a case for using the more flexible approach of conservation area legislation. Councils might declare tree conservation, management or work zones, where the loss of existing trees would have a major impact and in which owners would be required to serve notice of any work proposed on trees. Detailed town hall tree records would vanish.

FLOWERS

For a good many months of the year flowers add colour, life and vitality to the London scene. But the capital city could go much further and concentrate on the cultivation of one or more species on which to base a festival of flowers. The tulip attracts visitors to Holland and Ottawa, Canada, cherry blossom casts a magic spell for spring visitors to Washington DC. It would be marvellous if London could build up a reputation as the city of the rose for example, with wild roses encouraged on vacant sites, or even if it simply became the flowering city.

Visibility

Boroughs could help bring this about if, like Bromley, they were to concentrate their efforts, not on municipal gardens, but at road junctions and outside public conveniences, places which are highly visible by people going about their daily business rather than requiring a special excursion into official green areas.

Boxes and baskets

Flower boxes and baskets have become increasingly popular and contribute much to the immediate urban scene. Again the boroughs can encourage this trend. Westminster for example has been seeking traders in specified areas such as Bayswater, the Edgware and Harrow Roads and Covent Garden to sponsor the cost including the original installation, subsequent care and a plaque. The council's leaflet says that an organised and concerted campaign to provide plants and baskets in those places furthest removed from existing greenery could well be the first step on the way to attract new investment and new people to an area, reduce the incidence of vandalism, bring communities together and instill a sense of pride among residents and traders alike. Even if none of this were true, and it could well be, to try to make London the urban garden of England would still be a good idea.

While the London Tourist Board stages an annual London in Bloom competition, more local competitions between streets as well as individuals and firms could help create even more interest. A first-class incentive would of course be some remission of rates or poll tax.

COLOUR

A palette of pastels gives Chalcot Square much of its charm – but Camden's sign shows no sign of integration

Careful injection of colour can enhance drab buildings and streets and raise spirits whatever the weather. In parts of London contrasting stone strimmings relieve great brick mansion blocks. In others, owners of flat-fronted stucco terraces have used a palette of soft pastels to lift the physical and psychological environment.

Colour on rail bridges which cross roads at high level also make a striking difference. Councils often fund the extra cost of colour over above traditional battleship grey, sometimes with the help of paint company sponsorship. But organisations like British Rail, London Regional Transport and The British Waterways Board really should make this sort of contribution themselves to improve the London scene – and their image.

Developments, particularly in docklands, have shown the difference colour makes to buildings and even a service like the light railway. One reason for the general regret, if not anger, at the removal of old-style telephone kiosks was that they added – like guardsmen outside Buckingham Palace and the London bus – a touch of welcome brightness.

However, since it is so easy to give the community the colour equivalent of an overdose, it is worth emphasising that word 'touch'. While special features are frequently enhanced by paint and subsequent freshening is not too demanding on time or cash, a technicolour building backcloth could quickly prove wearying and aggressive and clash with London's character and climate. Even if the sky is often grey, the street surface almost always, few people would wish for whole streets of scarlet structures. However red paving, especially brick, can look good when the rain tumbles down. Some boroughs are now adding colour under foot but, judging

Brightly coloured doors help relieve the drabness of this east London estate – and one household at least understands the need for people to be able to read street numbers from afar

by the occasional piece of patchwork, all too often, it would seem, without any overall vision. Suddenly a few square yards of colour appear, at junctions for example, which simply create a curiously unsettling effect.

ART

Murals can add colour and impact to windowless facades

Just as pictures and ornaments can enhance a room, statues, sculpture, murals and fountains contribute individuality, vitality and interest to the outside of buildings, streets, squares and parks. They can also arouse curiosity, excite the spirit or stay the restless mind. No one can tell the magic spun by Peter Pan on children in Kensington Gardens or the impact of Sir Winston Churchill in Parliament Square, the spotlit repose of Neal Street's recumbent figure, the vigour of the Brixton high-level mural or the wonder of light patterns over South Bank as the wind activates the sculpture of coloured tubes. Works of art are an essential part of the civilised city. But as well as enhancing the quality of local life, they can also be used to increase its general attraction and become a sales tool for investment and tourism.

Percentage for the arts

In Portland, Oregon one per cent of the construction costs of new city or county structures, public works as well as buildings, is dedicated to the acquisition of visible works of art and high quality crafts. When hard times hit Seattle, that city also decided to devote one per cent of the city's capital improvement programme to public art, which has resulted over time in the purchasing and commissioning of literally hundreds of works including crafted manhole covers and attractive electricity sub-stations. More recently the Seattle Arts Commission involved five artists in the creation of a landscaped lakeside footway, one contribution being a sound garden with tall steel pipes which sing with the wind. Toronto requires a percentage for the arts including the special treatment of doors, buildings or pavements, quality seating, stained glass or a water feature, as well as more traditional art forms, in developments which involve rezoning. The city also holds competitions on prominent sites.

Artists in urban design

In North America generally artists have been brought in to look at whole areas, including buildings and pedestrian routes, to suggest ideas, not just for beautification but also for transforming a place and space. In Basildon a sculptress was called in to work with engineers on the design of the main entrance to the town including the detailed shaping of the subway, paving and planting. But it is still more usual for artists to be involved on individual projects such as community murals.

There are developers, who positively enjoy commissioning works of art or craft to enhance new buildings, and the establishment of a number of trusts and agencies has made it easier for the enthusiast with less confidence to find advice and informed help including the organisation of competitions.

Annual competitions

Westminster has promoted a sculpture competition and Kingston is incorporating a number of sculptures and murals in its new town centre relief road, in part using limited competitions. However there has been nothing as positive as the scheme in Gateshead which advertised nationally for ideas from artists, sculptors and craftworkers for ambitious and small-scale proposals for a considerable area along the south bank of the Tyne.

Bearing in mind the need for quality, London could benefit greatly from more new public art. If every borough commissioned or held a competition for one new work a year at a cost of say £25,000, in just one year the capital city would have 33 new works. In 10 years that figure would rise to 330. If the money were divided between a sculpture and a mural, in each case the figure would rise to 660 and there might

*Fountains and sculpture can add
enjoyment to looking round London*

be scope for a trail of new urban outdoor art. If boroughs focused their projects in one area, park or square, they could have the basis of a reasonable sculpture garden. They might also win contributions or commissions from local business or individuals and make that sculpture garden into a minor tourist attraction. If one year they all held competitions for mobile sculptures using light, there would be a new reason for enjoying London by night. Water and fountains might form another theme, floodlighting another. A Thames development authority could cooperate with boroughs and business to launch a series of works for specific sites along the river and create an outdoor museum of modern art.

Floodlighting

Floodlighting sets the city stage at night, enhancing the hidden beauty of buildings, great and normally insignificant, as light and shade emphasise the details of a facade. St. Paul's Cathedral, heavy by day, becomes almost etherial by night, as it floats above the surrounding roofs. The lighting on Tower Bridge has been redesigned and increased. Many buildings do enliven London by night – and make walking along those streets safer. Obviously people in residential areas do not want to be dazzled out of their sleep, but floodlighting within reasonable hours can enhance small offices, pubs, restaurants, gardens and bridges. For simple structures, it need not be expensive.

Public Statues Metropolis Act

There is however one small but niggling legislative anomaly which should be cleared up relating to new statues for London. Under the Public Statues Act of 1854 no public statue shall be erected in any public place without the written consent of commisioners. The said commisioners have long since gone but the act was never repealed and the Secretary of State for the Environment still has to give his consent for all figures (but not other forms of sculpture) in public places. Although the Department of the Environment sees this primarily as an opportunity for ensuring that there are arrangements for long-term maintenance, the close supervision of statues by central instead of local government does seem an unnecessary diversion of scarce time and resources.

Building details

Finally sculptures and fountains are not the only way to enliven and enhance London. Well-designed and crafted building details also make an individual and cumulative difference, as can be seen mainly in more historic parts of London, in doors, windows, railings, pediments and brick reliefs.

Well crafted details add to the character of the city

9 Ways and means

For many years following the second world war, London local government took the lead in rebuilding areas involved in the blitz, new highway construction, slum clearance and comprehensive redevelopment. Although the Greater London Council has come and gone and the boroughs are more infrequently major builders, councillors still represent areas of London and local town halls control much of the public highway framework, deal with planning applications, own and manage a good deal of housing, school and other open space, have powers to enhance the environment and can generally do a great deal for the good.

If the controlling party so chooses, quality of local London life can be placed at the top of the agenda. Traditionally engineers have tended to dominate the street scene introducing practical schemes to deal with traffic needs backed by substantial budgets and government legislation. Since street quality is generally less subject to precise measurement than speed and safety, a significant improvement of London's environment requires an equally significant shift of political will.

NEW COMMITTEE STRUCTURE

One method might be to add environment to the list of factors always to be considered in all decisions like finance or, in Labour-controlled councils, women and ethnic groups. A much better answer may lie in the creation of a special quality of environment committee under the chairmanship of the council leader or deputy served by the chief executive's department. This would emphasise its importance politically and mean that, within the hierarchy, other departments would have to respect that priority and play their parts regardless of possible professional jealousies. The fact that Westminster's leader has so obviously backed the borough's quality of life campaign undoubtedly makes all the difference within and without the council.

Another approach may be the creation of area committees with their own budgets, which again can be single-minded and insist on an input from the different departments. Greenwich for example set up three special development subcommittees reporting to policy and resources to cover the development and management of borough centres. The actual budgets have not been large but maintenance increased and it became easier to coordinate the contribution of different departments. The committee has also worked with local shopkeepers and individuals to achieve joint improvements.

SHOPPING AND RESIDENTIAL FORUMS

Generally there is increasing realisation of the need to work with as well as for different sections of the community, to set up some kind of regular forum for local shopping centres, to listen and act on the ideas of outside professionals and tradesmen and to encourage sponsorshp and other forms of financial contribution.

Similar principles should apply equally to residential areas but with street, neighbourhood and community associations normally creating their own impetus for improvement. Councils can encourage and set the framework in which they operate – for example Facelift in Southwark or the Brighter Borough fund in Kensington and Chelsea, built up originally with money from a lottery and now used to stimulate improvements including sharing the cost of quite small but cumulatively useful ideas such as the replacement of railings in squares.

TRUSTS AND COMPANIES LIMITED BY GUARANTEE

But action need not these days stem simply from traditional authority. As can be shown by only a few examples, trusts and companies limited by guarantee are increasingly active in improvement and change. Over a number of years, the North Kensington Amenity Trust has transformed an area under the elevated motorway with a network of workshops, shops, offices, sports, charitable and community facilities and a training centre. Nearly 20 per cent of the space has been set aside for commercial development to ensure the long-term financial viability of the whole.

At Waterloo, now that the public inquiry into alternative schemes is history, Coin Street Community Builders Ltd, a non-profit distributing company limited by guarantee, has again shown that local people can take responsibility for the management of major change.

In Thamesmead, Thamesmead Town was set up as a private company limited by guarantee, when the GLC was abolished, to continue and manage this equivalent of a new town development. While the local authorities of Greenwich and Bexley control most normal services, the company looks after open space, the cleaning of estate roads, the collection of bulk rubbish and new building. Except for confidential items board meetings are held in public and questions allowed from the floor. The nine areas each elect a member to the board.

In docklands a joint operation between the corporation, borough, Sports Council and a number of major companies to transform a former shed into a major indoor sports and exhibition centre has grown into a more substantial exercise with major private funding and management but still a trust to ensure use by local people for 65 per cent of the year.

The Heritage of London Trust has done valiant work in contributing to conservation projects all over London from the cleaning of church stonework to the restoration of cabmen's shelters.

In Covent Garden the Jubilee Hall Development Consortium was set up to ensure the retention of sports facilities and a regular street market in a project which blended conservation and new building. The traders raised the money for the rebuilding of the market and the sport hall by an ingenious scheme with individuals buying the freehold of their stalls for one or more days a week (from £3600 for just the one day). This produced £2,300,000 which, together with interest and profits during the period of construction, came to £3,000,000 interest-free upfront money. The consortium then worked in partnership with a developer who paid a premium for the head lease on the land and benefits from 12,000 square feet of offices.

In Richmond the local environment trust has bought a boathouse and created additional funds by selling timeshares in a boat for two days's use a month for 60 years.

In Tower Hamlets the local environment trust has coordinated improvements on more than 75 local sites including landscaping dereliction. It claims that one of the great advantages of working outside local government is the flexibility and ability to react to local people.

Amenity organisations

Amenity and civic groups also have great potential as an even more positive force for action than in the past, not simply criticising or campaigning but actually helping with the spadework of research, contributing professional skills and actual involvement in development. Weston-Super-Mare for example bought and restored its own property with the help of a number of grants and loans, including one from the Architectural Heritage Fund, and the use of Manpower Services Commission labour. Now the society not only has an office and a shop selling booklets, postcards and souvenirs but a special conservation bureau which advises people who might not think of using an architect on ways to repair, convert, improve and enhance older property in keeping with local style and ethos. That sort of service could help individuals and builders in many parts of London and include the thorny question of shop fronts. Weston-Super-Mare also salvages scarce building features and materials, and has worked with the MSC on local landscape, commissioned a feasibility study for converting a redundant church hall (again with MSC labour), raised money from the English Tourist Board and Carnegie UK Trust to produce a Weston-Super-Mare interpretation plan and published children's and local history trails, not to mention its own magazine six times a year.

If civic and amenity groups throughout London were to inform, advise, publish, campaign and carry out schemes in this way, they would begin to lose their image as well-heeled preservationists who hate hamburger chains and much else that is modern.

The media and information

The media too could play an enhanced role. With the tremendous growth of home ownership and housing as a major personal investment, property columns have become regular features. But there ought also to be scope, even in national newspapers and magazines, more regularly to cover architecture, design, potholes, clutter, litter and other issues relating to the urban affairs in which the capital's quality of life would come high on the agenda.

The assembly of more information on the legal and administrative background of the ways such problems are tackled in major cities in other countries could also be useful.

A NEW LONDON WATCHDOG

However while this collection of ways and means could contribute to improvement in the capital, there is a major gap on the London scene – the lack of a really effective body campaigning and caring for the capital. And of course, since the Greater London Council was abolished without any replacement, there is no proper political forum in which to discuss ideas and issues, to air controversial development schemes, debate the need for height restrictions in sensitive areas and consider such problems and opportunities as increasing tourism, to name only a few relevant subjects.

Parliament takes all too little interest. Although London Members form a substantial group, they rarely act together to bring major topics to the fore and, if they do, any debate tends to take place late into the night. While Wales and Scotland have their own Secretaries of State, London, with more people than either and as many, if not more, problems and potential, has no minister. The person nearest this description is the Secretary of State for the Environment who has supreme responsibility for all other English cities as well, not to mention, local government and planning.

The 32 London boroughs and the City Corporation vie with each other like so many Italian principalities and consider the impact of development as it concerns their local pride, purse and particular interests. The Labour-controlled boroughs have long departed from the London Boroughs Association, which means there are now two rival groups for exchanging information and ideas. In days of yore, members and officers managed to talk, sometimes agree with one another and even press for necessary change.

The London Planning Advisory Committee brings together one political member for each borough and operates with a small staff based in Romford, Essex (which most Londoners probably scarcely think of as part of the great capital). Created after the GLC's demise, this organisation has been working hard on key strategic issues but has yet to show political teeth or clout – even if it can. The London Docklands Development Corporation, which controls the future of eight square miles from the City through to the proposed East London river crossing, is not even a member and has flouted established London manners and practice, for example with respect to London's existing high buildings policy.

With such fragmentation, there seems an obvious need for at least some form of London watchdog to gather information, ensure debate of the more important schemes and issues and to produce ideas for the positive improvement of the capital city. It is astonishing that such an organisation does not already exist, ideally run with the zest and zeal of Save Britain's Heritage but much more widely based and interested for example in the economic, social and environmental impact of new development and trends, particularly with respect to the central area, which most people regard as the capital. It might even galvanise an exhibition showing the location and details of the most important proposals in the pipeline.

A LONDON CONFEDERATION

There is room too for a more august, official body or forum to ensure that London's interests remain to the fore. In North America, major cities tend to produce groups of business men and women who take an interest in the development, management, image and marketing of the urban area. In Baltimore just such a group decided many years ago to begin to restore their home town's slumping fortunes by commissioning a first-class planner and then working alongside an organisation deliberately set up at arm's length from the mayor and city hall. Glasgow has set up an organisation called Glasgow Action with 12 founding members from business plus the principal of Strathclyde University and representatives from Glasgow District and Strathclyde Regional Councils.

Again Leicester, faced with the need for new jobs and the threat of lost prosperity through out-of-town shopping, has also applied itself with real purpose to create cooperation and trust between business and local government. As well as a 10-year action programme and a budget for environmental improvements (nearly £600,000 in 1987/88), the city set up a retail consultative panel in 1984 including local politicians and business people to concentrate on the quality and attractiveness of the city. Three sub-groups look after environmental improvements, traffic, transport and parking and publicity and promotion. Issues range widely from litter collection to major planning applications and events. Planners are heavily involved in promotion and plan road races, festivals and fairs and 10 major companies and the city have contributed £6000 each to establish an advertising fund. This approach has helped different strands in the city to pull together, put their best foot forward and work towards a place in which people want to be.

London has little to offer other than the London Chamber of Commerce and Industry, the London Enterprise Agency and the London Tourist Board, none of which fill the same bill. Although the latter has a definite interest in the management and development of the environment, old and new, its role is restricted. The other two are basically concerned with business. London needs the urban equivalent of the Confederation of British Industry – London Looks Forward or London 2000 – which promotes, campaigns and rewards. The Greater Indianapolis Progress Committee has 350 members. A London campaign might make do with somewhat fewer. But it could, in the manner of the Baltimore is Best competitions, stage Londonwide annual awards for people who have contributed to the improvement of the city including ideas and achievements by individuals, architects, developers, local government, trusts, amenity societies and community action groups. A dinner could take place somewhere like Guildhall, the winners announced on the spot and the occasion run with the panache of the Booker prize as a significant social event.

ARCHITECTURAL ADVISORY COMMITTEE

It would be useful if the capital, at least for the central area, developed for more important schemes some form of regular architectural advisory committee. In the United States such committees offer the opportunity, not simply for criticism but also the injection of constructive thinking at a reasonably early stage by a number of outsiders with development as well as professional expertise. While in many respects the Royal Fine Art Commission fulfils this function, its contribution might be put on a more formal basis with a group of commissioners who are known to be concentrating on the London scene. As an American example Portland has a development commission, which not only vets all development (speedily) but has set aims including architectural excellence and the improvement of the pedestrian environment with additional shops at street level to liven the scene, even in public buildings such as law courts and the town hall.

LONDON CAPITAL DEVELOPMENT AGENCY

Finally the capital needs some form of organisation, ad hoc commission or corporation possibly, to galvanise or coordinate improvement schemes which are of London as opposed to borough importance. Other capital cities have special planning commissions. The urban development corporation provides a useful precedent and could be used to create a London Capital Development Agency spinning off small agencies for specific projects ranging for example from the Improvement of London's Gateways, such as the M4 from Heathrow to Piccadilly (perhaps new landscaping, banners and better cleaning), railway stations and the Victoria bus arrival terminal which has neither information nor proper facilities, to East London Revitalisation, the Reclamation of Derelict Land or the Transformation of the Thames.

The people and organisations of London, and their leaders, can go about their business and pleasure, ignore the all too obvious degradation, accept the insidious erosion of the environment and only complain about physical urban decline to their friends. Or they can become more responsible and responsive within their own communities at work and home and create pressure for change – by government, national and local, which means them, too.

Cities do not, any more than gardens, look after themselves. Without work, care and attention, paving cracks, paint chips, untrimmed shrubs and rampant weeds block paths and views and flowers and framework are destroyed. If this urban garden is unkempt, overgrown and gives displeasure, it is surely time to consider changes in methods, management and style. There is a choice. Increasing public squalor? Or a new look for London and a more livable city?

10 Detailed recommendations

I. LITTER DISGRACE

The Government should:

1. Investigate with industry the possible imposition of cash deposits on the sale of cans of drinks and bottles.
2. Consider a more concerted drive to raise awareness of the effect of litter on people's lives and ways of re-educating society.
3. Look into ways for speeding up the removal of abandoned cars and the clearance of visible litter and rubble from privately owned land.
4. Sort out the responsibility for ensuring the cleanliness of London's waterways, foreshore, banks and towpaths.

London boroughs should:

1. Provide large numbers of well-designed litter bins with the help of business, individual and community sponsorship.
2. Provide large containers at regular intervals at street corners in areas subject to dumped sacks of litter.
3. Try to agree conditions on proposals for takeaway food outlets to make proprietors responsible for the cleanliness of the pavement in the immediate vicinity.
4. Encourage business – or residential – sponsorship of additional street sweepers.
5. Consider removing business waste in return for a commitment or contract to keep pavements well swept. This principle could be extended to residential areas in return for a reduction in rates or community charge.
6. Ensure that litter bins, street containers and bottle banks are regularly emptied and maintained and consider the use of mobile telephones so that management reacts more quickly to remove nascent litter dumps.
7. Consider the use of clean teams or city chars with distinctive smart clean uniforms and carts.
8. Appoint someone with specific responsibility for litter abatement and the encouragement of litter watch schemes.
9. Consider the introduction of a litter warning system backed by fixed penalty tickets.
10. Consider grouping environmental enforcement officers to form an urban improvement or patrol force.

11. Campaign against litter including the distribution of information to all properties about collection days and times with hotline telephone numbers for complaints, inquiries and ideas. Shopkeepers and local residents should be encouraged to act as the council's eyes and ears to provide information about the build-up of problems.

12. Prosecute individuals and organisations dumping litter in public places and publicise details of successful convictions.

13. Actively involve schools in anti-litter educational drives and actual clean-ups.

14. Consider regular, possibly monthly, collections of bulky items which people are allowed to place on the pavement the previous night to allow others to remove articles which seem useful. The occasional placing of well publicised skips is a possible but less convenient alternative.

15. Ensure that company chief executives are informed about badly maintained local branch properties.

Other:

1. A competition should be held, possibly under Design Council auspices, to promote the design of better-looking storage for household refuse and for street corner containers.

2. More shopkeepers, particularly in fast food, should undertake to look after the area outside properties and incidentally improve their image. Other occupiers including residents should once again assume more personal responsibility for their section of the public footpath or highway.

3. Fines relating to litter and dumping should be high enough to deter and costs sufficient to cover the real expense of public prosecution. The same principle applies on a much higher scale to flytipping and include the cost of removal of rubble.

4. Local media could raise public consciousness of litter and bring problem areas to the attention of careless and/or absentee owners.

5. Supermarkets should consider the introduction of deposit systems for trolleys.

6. London Regional Transport should give every underground station a regular spring-clean, make daily cleaning more visible and provide and regularly empty more litter bins.

2 MORE SCRUFF AND DIRT

The Government should:

1. Consider enabling magistrates to relate community service more directly to environmental crimes and also involve younger graffiti offenders, and perhaps their

parents, in cleaning up operations.

2. Enable local authorities to recover the costs of the removal of flyposted advertisements.

3. Consider the needs of London's visitors in deciding on maintenance programme for important public monuments.

4. Ensure that statutory undertakers are made fully responsible for the speedy proper reinstatement of the public highway and footpath on a temporary as well as permanent basis and for the payment of any inspectorate to check on the quality of their work.

5. Make dog owners responsible for removal of faeces from public places.

6. Enable councils to impose the screening of building and refurbishment sites immediately fronting pavements as a normal planning or building condition.

London boroughs should:

1. Consider the potential of blank walls for murals, posters and climbing plants to avoid graffiti. An experimental graffiti wall might be worthwhile.

2. Consider the introduction of controlled circuit television into more subways to help deter vandals, increase the likelihood of successful prosecution and enhance personal security.

3. Impose conditions against flyposting in granting entertainment licences.

4. Consider the provision of community hoardings or poster sites and the award of temporary licences to sites which attract flyposting.

5. Consider the introduction of considerate contractor schemes.

6. Consider more economic charges for the use of the public highway by building skips.

Other:

1. London Regional Transport should fill empty poster sites and consider letting suitable space or kiosks at underground interchanges and on platforms to small shopkeepers.

2. Owners of dirty buildings should consider the advantages of cleaning their facades.

3. Contractors could improve their image as well as the environment of building sites by painting simple bands of paint or even murals on hoardings and including drawings and descriptions of schemes.

4. Owners of bridges used by roosting pigeons should accept responsibility for removing dirt where it endangers or offends members of the public.

3 CLUTTER – MAINLY OFFICIAL

The Government should:

1. Issue regular Department of Transport circulars relating to environmental quality of the footpath environment, the need for less hardware and the importance of regular assessment of the overall impact of accumulated ad-hoc additions under highway regulations.

2. Enable councils to declare areas in which estate agency boards are banned and to remove estate agents's boards from properties with more than one board to storage, for return to owners only on payment of the full cost of removal and storage.

3. Consider the pros and cons of a more commercial approach to the use of the public footpath for regular commercial purposes.

London boroughs should:

1. Appoint an officer with design qualifications to vet the need, style and location of all additional objects on the public footpath.

2. Select one or more streets as demonstration projects aimed at reducing the number of street signs and generally reconsider the need for other pavement clutter.

3. Seek to involve local amenity societies in a census of current street hardware and joint working parties on ideas for improvement. These could include:

the elimination or reduction in width and colour intensity of yellow lines and flashings;

the relocation of parking meters to the back of pavements or, still better, their replacement with a smaller number of pay and display ticket machines;

the need for bollards and guard rails;

the use of buildings for street lighting fixtures;

the grouping of signs and their possible attachment to walls, railings or bollards;

the desirability and location of street advertising

the design, number, colour and location of items such as litter, salt and grit bins, bottle banks and automatic public conveniences;

the visibility and cleanliness of street names and numbers of shops as well as homes;

the aftercare of planters.

Other:

1. Magistrates should award higher fines and costs for parking on pavements.

4 STREET FACELIFTS

The Government should:

1. Leave the choice of colour for highway signposts to local decision.

London boroughs should:

1. Allocate a regular budget to environmental improvement and create rolling programmes dedicated to achieve general upgrading over a set period of time.
2. Insist on the provision of more stylish and sensibly located bus shelters, particularly where advertising is involved.
3. Give careful consideration to the design of guard rails and other public highway objects.
4. Allow and encourage pubs, cafes and restaurants to erect temporary glass-sided structures on the footpath in winter.
5. Encourage the creation with different interests of joint local forums and set up joint projects with local groups, organisations and property owners sharing costs such as professional urban design studies and the implementation of street facelifts. Local interests should also help decide priorities.
6. Apply the principles of cooperation and cost sharing to the upgrading of small parades and individual shops.
7. Make contact with absentee owners of empty property to ensure they are aware of its potential.
8. Look into ways of encouraging the use of empty flats over shops.
9. Consider the conversion of suitable empty shops to housing or offices and of some flats on vandalised estates to offices, small business or other use.
10. Allow the more American style of strip development on major arterial routes.
11. Organise and attract sponsors for local annual competitions for urban design and street improvements.

Other:

1. Street trading associations should consider taking the lead and commission their own improvement schemes. They might also consider the appointment of town centre managers, similar to those employed in covered centres under single ownership, to coordinate and look after cleanliness, security, promotion and events. Such a move should qualify for some reduction in rates or community charge.
2. Local media should campaign to persuade property owners – absentee or local – of the need to let vacant commercial and residential property.
3. An annual Londonwide competition should be launched for urban design projects.

5 PRIORITY FOR PEOPLE

The Government should:

1. Consider giving local authorities full control over parking.
2. Overhaul responsibility for parking enforcement.
3. Consider legislation to allow for the creation within towns and cities of areas in

which people have legal priority over cars and the introduction of different lower speed limits for different parts of the built-up area.

London boroughs should: 1. Consider the introduction of more speed humps, traffic chokes, the enlargement of pavements at the entrances to side streets, the insertion of central strips at junctions, the more general widening of pavements, the use of the chicane to slow down traffic speed and planting trees in the road instead of the footpath.
2. Experiment with temporary road closures for specific times in the day, days in the week or for a period of the year, for example to allow restaurants to spread onto the street in the summer months or to enhance shopping conditions at Christmas or during the sales.
3. Increase pedestrian crossing times at traffic lights.
4. Improve the environment and safety of subways.
5. Experiment with new forms of parking control.

6 SPACE IN THE CITY

London boroughs should: 1. Try to use section 52 agreements for the creation and management of new open space.
2. See if there is scope for setting up companies with other local land owners to create new landscaped infrastructure.
3. Draw on the ideas, good will and involvement of local residents in both creation and management of new open space.
4. Act in an enabling role and provide a programme of events for volunteers.
5. Consider the introduction of city meadows, scented plants and fruit trees.
6. Consider the use of a park for an evolving exhibition of different approaches to the traditional London garden.
7. Promote the improvement and signing, by companies, trusts and voluntary groups as well as by themselves, of well mapped walks to link, not just open spaces, but areas and buildings of interest and historic and architectural merit.
8. Encourage the provision of plaques on buildings to provide capsules of local history.

Other: 1. Map publishers should consider the market for maps which cover the whole of Greater London.

110

7 THE THAMES FOR PLEASURE

The Government should:

1. Set up a Thames Development Authority to coordinate and promote the river and attractions alongside as a major new leisure park embracing art, history, entertainment, education, sport, shopping and open space. Its objectives should include:

> the development of more places to eat and drink overlooking the river;
> public access to the water's edge and the establishment of the proposed long-distance Thames path;
> a rolling programme of investment in hard and soft landscape;
> competitions for the improvement of specific sites such as the Greenwich foot tunnel;
> other improvements and events such as floodlighting, the encouragement of open-air art, the introduction of a giant computerised screen and regular Thames fairs.

2. Consider using Britain's next international garden festival to transform a derelict Thamesside site into an urban laboratory concentrating on different types of open space.

Other:

1. The tourist trade should be encouraged to develop all-day tours using special river transport as an alternative to coaches.

8 TREES, FLOWERS, COLOUR AND ART

The Government should:

1. Review legislation relating to tree preservation orders.
2. Set an example to private organisations by contributing a percentage of all building contracts to the enhancement of the environment with publicly visible arts or crafts.
3. Repeal the Public Statues Metropolis Act.

London boroughs should:

1. Seek the agreement of local people to look after new trees, including the cleaning of shrub and plant containers.
2. Work with the London Tourist Board for the promotion of a flower for London to enhance the capital's image as a flowering city.
3. Plant flowers in highly visible locations, not simply parks.
4. Encourage the sponsorship of hanging flower baskets and additional window boxes through competitions within streets and possibly some remission of rates or community charge.

5. Encourage the sensitive use of colour.

6. Consider the sponsorship of annual competitions for outdoor works of art including fountains, floodlighting and sculpture, which might eventually create art trails and parks. They should also encourage crafted building details.

Other:

1. A conference should be organised to exchange information and ideas about trees.

2. London Regional Transport and British Rail should accept a greater environmental role and help create a brighter London.

9 WAYS AND MEANS

The Government should:

1. Consider the establishment of ad-hoc single-minded development authorities to achieve special improvements which involve more than one borough.

London boroughs should:

1. Consider setting up a special committee under the council's leader or deputy leader to concentrate attention on the environment. An alternative approach would be to set up committees responsible for small segments of a borough.

2. Establish local forums in both commercial and residential areas to open up avenues for new ideas including sponsorship and self-help.

Other:

1. Amenity societies should consider expanding their activities to include, for example, development, advice on conversion of local property, the sale of architectural features and the preparation of local interpretation plans.

2. The media could help improve the look of London by encouraging more awareness and raising its importance in political terms.

3. London needs a watchdog organisation to gather information about development and change, galvanise public debate and produce ideas for the positive improvement of the capital.

4. London also needs an organisation to bring together business and other interests to concentrate on the improvement and promotion of London. It could stage highly publicised annual awards for people and organisations which have contributed to the improvement of the capital.

5. There should be some form of architectural advisory committee to encourage excellence in London development.

Appendix

LIST OF ORGANISATIONS CONSULTED

Barking and Dagenham
Barnet
Brent
Bromley
Camden
City of London
City of Westminster
Croydon
Greenwich
Hammersmith and Fulham
Havering
Hounslow
Kensington and Chelsea
Kingston-upon-Thames
Lewisham
Redbridge
Richmond
Southwark
Sutton
Tower Hamlets
Wandsworth

Department of the Environment
Department of Transport

British Waterways Board
Countryside Commission
Design Council
English Heritage
Leicester City Council
London Chamber of Commerce and
    Industry
London Docklands Development
    Corporation

London Museum
London Planning Advisory Committee
London Regional Transport
London Research Centre
London Tourist Board
London Waste Regulation Authority
Port of London Authority
Royal Institute of British Architects

British American Arts Association
Campaign to Improve London's
    Transport
City Art
Civic Trust
Coin Street Community Builders
Free Form
Friends of the Earth
Growth Unlimited
Heritage of London Trust
Inner London Juvenile Courts
Keep Britain Tidy Group
London Amenity and Transport
    Association
London Regional Passengers Committee
London Wildlife Trust
North Kensington Amenity Trust
Public Art Development Trust
Thamesmead Trust
Tower Hamlets Environment Trust
Town and Country Planning Association
UK 2000

ATTACKS
ON CHILD
RIOTS
RUBBISH
EVERYWHE
YOUR
SOCIETY
IS
FALLING
APART
Bull
Shit